# Chef
# Harry
# &
# Friends

To Claudia!
Best Always.
Harry

# Chef Harry & Friends

## *Sharing the Joys of the Table*

Chef Harry Schwartz

Sourcebooks
Inc.

Naperville, IL

Copyright © 1997 by Harry Schwartz
Cover Design by FineLine Marketing and Design / Scott Theisen, Sourcebooks, Inc.
Front Cover Photography by Kallan Nishimoto
Pasta by Cafferata, Richmond, CA
Back Cover Photography by Danny Sanchez
Internal Design by Andrew Sardina, Sourcebooks, Inc.

Published by Sourcebooks
P.O. Box 372
Naperville, Illinois 60566
(630) 961-3900
FAX: 630-961-2168

Naperville, IL

**Library of Congress Cataloging-in-Publication Data**
Schwartz, Harry.
    Chef Harry and friends: sharing the joys of the table / by Chef Harry Schwartz.
            p.      cm.
    Includes indexes.
    ISBN 1-57071-160-7 (pbk. : alk. paper)
            1. Cookery.   I. Title.
    TX714.H368    1997
    641.5—dc21                                                    97-14625
                                                                 CIP

Printed and bound in the United States of America.

10   9   8   7   6   5   4   3   2   1

This book is dedicated to those who believed that I could accomplish my dreams and helped me do so. I am fortunate that this list is very long and that those on it know who they are.

But most of all, I am forever dedicating my accomplishments to my loving wife. I am who I am because because she loves me. Lots of love also to my daughter, Alexa, and mother, as they have been great inspiration.

I must also, however, thank: Mr. Roger Ailes for believing in me right from the beginning—he waved the magic wand that got me in the door at NBC's *Today* show; my publicist, John Blanchette of Dale C. Olson & Associates who is my personal dream maker; Judy Martin who got this book deal for me with the help of John Kremer at New Horizons; and my invaluable friend, Garna Greenwald. There is no way to thank Antoinette, Katie, Matt, Al, Ann, Bryant, and all the crew at *Today*.

And finally, a special word of thanks to Lona and Henry Wolfe, not only for loving and supporting me for most of my life, but for showing me how to make anyone from any walk of life feel welcome in their home at all times. (And no one else I have ever known can stock a bar like Henry Wolfe!)

# Table of Contents

Introduction . . . . . . . . . . . . . . . . . . . . . . . ix

No Recipes Yet! . . . . . . . . . . . . . . . . . . . . 1

Sonoma Supper with the Tommy
    Smothers Family . . . . . . . . . . . . . . . . 9

Santa Fe Fete . . . . . . . . . . . . . . . . . . . . . . 17

Lunch at Shambala with Tippi Hedron
    and Friends . . . . . . . . . . . . . . . . . . . . 23

Festive Fall Celebration . . . . . . . . . . . . . . . 31

Centered Cuisine with Deepak Chopra . . . 37

Low Country Style Eats . . . . . . . . . . . . . . . 43

Picnic on the Beach with JoBeth Williams
    and Family . . . . . . . . . . . . . . . . . . . . . 51

A Healthful Holiday Breakfast . . . . . . . . . . . 57

Low Fat Southwestern for Geraldo Rivera . . . . 63

Spicy Summer Supper . . . . . . . . . . . . . . . . 73

Thai Hollywood Holiday Banquet with
    Downtown Julie Brown . . . . . . . . . . . . . 79

Slim South of the Border Fiesta . . . . . . . . . . 87

Serious Supper for Funny Phyllis Diller . . . . . . 93

Picnic by the Pool . . . . . . . . . . . . . . . . . . 101

South African Holiday Supper with James
    Earl Jones . . . . . . . . . . . . . . . . . . . . . 107

Thanksgiving Leftover Makeover . . . . . . . . . 117

A Circus of a Meal with Ringling Brothers and

Barnum & Bailey . . . . . . . . . . . . . . . . . 123

A Sunday Evening Supper on the Veranda . . . . . . . . . . . 127

An Italian Style Vegetarian Feast. . . . . . . . . . . . . . . . 133

All Aboard with Gary Coleman. . . . . . . . . . . . . . . . 139

Maine Coast Respite . . . . . . . . . . . . . . . 147

A Legendary Meal for Legend Terry Moore . . . . . . . . . . . 153

Asian Delight . . . . . . . . . . . . . . . . . . . . . . . 161

Italian Love Fest with Renee Taylor and

Joseph Bologna . . . . . . . . . . . . . . . . . 169

The Perfect Shower . . . . . . . . . . . . . . . . . . . . . 181

Picnic on the "Almost" Lawn with Connie Stevens . . . . . . . . 187

Malibu Style Latke Fest. . . . . . . . . . . . . . . . . . . . 197

Dinner on the Dume with Jackie Zeman Gordon . . . . . . . . . 203

Seaside Supper on the Grill . . . . . . . . . . . . . . . . . 213

Coochi Coochi Ribs in Reno with Charro . . . . . . . . . . . . 219

Standing Room Only: The Cocktail Buffet . . . . . . . . . . . 223

Index of Recipes

By Course. . . . . . . . . . . . . . . . . . . . . 231

A–Z . . . . . . . . . . . . . . . . . . . . . 237

# Introduction

This book exemplifies that dreams do come true. I have always loved to cook and eat, and entertaining became a way for me to have a social life and make friends. Becoming an author, columnist, and television personality at thirty-nine took some major efforts and was not without many setbacks and frustrations. Through it all, I never stopped enjoying the process of creating environments in which to entertain our friends and family. Creating environments is what entertaining is all about. It is much more than food. Sharing this fun and my experiences with readers and viewers is a joy that comes as a by-product of doing what I love to do.

Feeding someone a meal merely requires serving them food. *Entertaining* someone means:

- creating an atmosphere that makes a guest comfortable with the surroundings

- putting together interesting people

- providing pleasing food and refreshments in an attractive manner

- caring for the needs of your guests

Sound tough? It couldn't be easier—or more fun.

*Introduction*

I consider entertaining a selfish endeavor because it brings me a great deal of pleasure. I start by creating the environment. A simple rose in a sugar bowl can change an end table. A small branch from a flowering tree or bush set in a marble-filled vase can dramatically change a room. Placing a potted flower for view as people arrive sets a pleasing tone. Candlelight is always a quick and easy mood setter, and a simple oil lamp can turn dinner outdoors into dinner al fresco. It does not have to take a lot of time or money, just a little thought and creativity. Just look around your cupboards, attic, basement, and garage, and put your imagination to work!

Because I helped set the table as a child, I have always appreciated beautiful china, crystal, and silver. Equally pleasing is collecting more casual and eclectic pieces for less formal entertaining. Blending these things with family heirlooms can result in a charming and warm environment. Setting the table and mixing things from old and new is a way to reflect on loving memories and gives the sense that each gathering is not only a culinary experience, but a joyous celebration.

Now for the food. The food experience stimulates at least four senses, if not all five. As your guests arrive, the chances are very good that they will smell what's cookin'. Before they eat it, they will see it. Already, without taking a bite, your guests have experienced your creations with two of their senses. Now they are ready to taste for their third sense's review, and they will also feel the food, at least with their tongue and palate. How smooth was that cheesecake? How velvety the chocolate sauce? How delicate the texture of the crust?

But, hearing the food, you ask? I won't mention the obvious breakfast cereal with a snap, crackle, and you know what else. But how about: sizzling rice soup, frying chicken, or the crunch of a crispy yam chip? Even the popping of a cork from the bottle of a good champagne is a culinary sense stimulator. And how many times have you heard, "My, that recipe sure sounds good"?

Entertaining is really not complicated, and you shouldn't make it so. If it sounds like work, step back and consider what you have planned. It will only seem like work when it is not well-planned, or when the plan is unmanageable with your current resources. Choose a formula for the food, flowers, and decor that is manageable, even if you blend in a few items from a caterer or gourmet market.

The entire process gets easier and becomes more fun with each experience. If an event is really important to you, never experiment with new dishes or untried techniques. Go for what you know so you can relax and be comfortable, not only during the event, but for the days and hours before. Add a sprig of rosemary to that pot roast, and serve it with marinated grilled vegetables, your favorite salad, and maybe a luscious chocolate-mousse cake done by the French bakery down the road. Arrange a sprig of thyme or an edible flower on each plate. Your guests will think you just got back from the Cordon Bleu! Keep it fun. We are talking about a meal, not a life challenge.

### Introduction

Most of the recipes in this book are quite easy. Many can be done in advance or prepared to near final stages ahead of time. I am always a guest at my own parties. Plan menus so you can be part of the group rather that sweating in the kitchen. Set the table a night or two in advance and prepare the bar as much as a week before the event. Anything that can be done ahead of time prevents rushing later. Never forget that each day, no matter how many people are expected, is a day that can be shared with a friend or loved one. Life is too short to sweat over a party. The first chapter of this book will go into much more detail about planning.

Lastly, remember that sitting down to a good meal with loved ones stimulates your ever-present desire to express appreciation for your beautiful life. We are all surrounded by a beautiful world that provides us with beautiful things to enjoy and share. All of us have so many reasons to be thankful. Each of the menus in this book will present words that we can use as toasts or expressions of our thankfulness for our beautiful lives. Culinary creations are food for the stomach. Laughter is food for the heart. Appreciation is food for the soul.

# No Recipes Yet!

If you are just starting to entertain, you may not yet know the importance of planning. If you have experience, by now planning may be second nature. In any case, planning ahead and thinking about the processes involved in having a party is what makes the difference between work and play. With today's busy lifestyles, I find I have pockets of time here and there when I can devote to certain elements involved in the process. What's first?

Make a quick list that contains the answers to the following questions (I do a subconscious version of this for every meal, even school lunches for my daughter. Planning saves time!):

- purpose of the event

- date and time of event

- who is coming

- invitations (if needed)

- menu

- flowers and/or decorations (if desired)

- entertainment (if desired)

- service persons, i.e., bartenders, valet parkers, service help, clean up (if needed)

## PURPOSE OF EVENT

From a bag lunch for school to a dream wedding, we must determine
the purpose of the event. This is the reason for the process to exist.
This determines the rest.

## DATE AND TIME OF EVENT

These will certainly have an impact on the menu and the guest
list. If invitations other than those by telephone are involved,
there must be enough time in advance for designing, printing,
addressing, and delivery.

Sometimes it's fun to pick an odd time for a party, like a Saturday
afternoon picnic for families instead of a cocktail party for adults
only. Have a holiday open house on a Sunday afternoon. Some
guests come and stay only a few minutes, and others stay all day.
Set out a buffet, talk, and have fun. It could start one of the great
traditions of the years to come.

## WHO IS COMING

When my wife and I began entertaining together, sometimes,
right before a party was about to start in our living room, we
would think to ourselves, "Are we crazy to be putting this group
of people together in one room?!?" But you never have a bad party
when you limit your friends to nice people. That way, there is
never a risk in putting them all together in one room!

# INVITATIONS

Invitations are not always needed, especially for smaller, less formal events. But I like to make invitations even for casual entertaining simply because I enjoy it. I have many colors of sealing waxes for envelopes, and I always buy attractive stationery when I see it on sale. With a gold pen, some sealing wax, and a little imagination, you can make some wonderful invitations. If this is your bag, then fine. If not, and you are having an event that requires invitations, establish a budget, meet with someone who will help create them with you, and have them printed. Some companies will even address and mail invitations for you. With a lower budget, try a copy store or a friend with a computer and printer. You will be amazed by what can be produced.

For a wedding, you may want a calligrapher to address the envelopes. If you or your spouse is a computer buff, you can make your own invitations and laser print the envelopes in your choice of hundreds of available fonts (type styles).

Paper selections are immense for custom invitation, as are pre-printed boxed and ready to go ensembles. We have a dear friend, Georgeann Kuhl, of Harpswell, Maine, who makes stunning paper by hand. She incorporates natural elements like leaves, flowers, herbs, and shells, as well as recycled fabrics, into her product. They make stunning invitations. Touches like this make an event special, even a dinner party for a few friends.

Party invitations should be received at least two weeks in advance. Invitations for weddings and more formal events should be received at least thirty days before the occasion. In today's world of communications, you can fax or email your invitations for that office party and have some Internet fun.

## MENU

We are finally talking about food! As you peruse the pages of this book, you will see that I have presented a series of menus from many different types of events, some of them are even star studded as seen on my public television show *Chef Harry & Friends*! None of these menus should be considered "fixed." Please use your imagination to mix and match recipes and have some fun. Unless you are baking, feel free to alter spice and flavoring amounts (more or less garlic, ginger, etc.) to suit your tastes. Pick food that fits the following conditions that only you can determine:

- Theme or time of event
- Guests who will be eating your food
- How the food is to be served, i.e., sit down, buffet, or formally
- How much you have budgeted to spend on the food and beverages
- How much time you have to prepare the food
- Technical restraints: oven, refrigerator, and work space

Be honest with yourself here, as it is very important to enjoying your own party. Do not hesitate to pull out recipes that freeze well and add them to the menu if serving a lot of people. That way, you can begin well in advance. If you find you can not do it all, order two dozen spring rolls from your favorite Chinese restaurant, and make your own dipping sauce, for example. A quality local fish market that will boil up large cocktail shrimp for you can save your life when Aunt Sarah lets you know the morning of the party that she is bringing four friends "you will just love" along with her. Never a problem to the chef on his or her feet, just quick solutions and a phone call or two. I look at more people in my home as a wider audience to exhibit my skills!

Do not be ashamed to use a caterer to help you out. Maybe something came up and your time allotments have to change, so make your own appetizers and dessert, and buy the rest, or vice versa. Finding a caterer with whom you are comfortable, food and budget wise, is a valuable asset to any entertainer. When it is time for an event that you do not want to tackle, you will know you have someone on whom you can depend.

Once you have established your menu based on your own personal and practical formula, it is time to make some more lists. First, put the menu down on paper. Anything that you are not making yourself should have the name and phone number of who is making it for you right next to it so you do not have to look up the number to order, confirm, reconfirm, and call just before picking up to confirm again.

Next, put together a comprehensive shopping list. If more than one store is in the picture, separate the list by store. Then, separate the main grocery list by department so you only go down each aisle once. I save my produce and baked goods until last so they do not get squashed! Any ingredients that are not perishable and are packaged for a long shelf life should be worked into earlier trips to the store and kept in one place in the pantry. This holds for the beverages as well. That way, when it is time to buy the perishable goods, half of your shopping is already done. (Make sure everyone in your house knows what is off limits!)

When it is time to begin the preparations, look at your recipes and prepare like ingredients all at once. For instance, chop enough onions for all the recipes that use chopped onion and have it ready in a zipper lock bag. Mince a bunch of fresh garlic and put it in a jar, pouring olive or safflower oil over the top. Cover the jar tightly, and it will keep in the refrigerator for up to a week. Use your food processor with a plan. Process parsley first, then basil, then oregano, then onions, and lastly garlic. This order means a quick scraping between each ingredient instead of that painful disassembly and full washing each time (yuck). Soon you will understand why some people enjoy cooking and others find it work.

## FLOWERS AND DECORATIONS

We really enjoy having flowers in our home. I always look for sales on orchids and African violets, as they can make center-pieces for many events. Establishing yourself with a florist is essential if you want flowers around. If you are a good customer, you can often get a discount, have special flowers held for you, and get gifts of small supplies like raffia and an occasional floral oasis (that block of foam that holds water, which you stick flowers in and they stay put). I have learned a great deal from many florists over the years, and my tables have benefited from them.

Many towns have farmers' markets where fresh flowers can be very inexpensive. You do not need a degree to put flowers in a vase. Just cut the stems and put them in water. Fresh and natural is always classic. Seven lily stems in a simple glass vase with a raffia bow is elegant, inexpensive, and quick. If carefully picked, fresh flowers can last a week or more and add beauty to your bedroom or entry after they have served you well on the dining room table.

With decorations, the sky is the limit. For most occasions, nothing is needed besides a few flowers. For larger events, you can blow up a few balloons or hire a professional and spend a fortune. I often borrow from my daughter's shell collection and scatter the table with a few when serving shellfish. Fresh evergreen from the tree in the yard can be artfully laid on the table for beauty and scent. Money is not always the issue, creativity is.

Here is another piece of the puzzle that can be assembled in advance. Arrange the flowers and decorations a day or two in advance. It makes the party last longer for you and makes it easier too!

## ENTERTAINMENT

This is not always necessary and can range in cost from free to very expensive. My daughter loves ballet, and many times, I have sat down at the piano and played while she dances and sings for our guests. From ponies at a birthday party to a video DJ, entertainment can make or break a party. Be your own judge and check out anyone you plan to hire with previous customers. Make sure to get all agreements in writing.

## SERVICE PERSONS

Budget and the number of people are the biggest considerations here. I love to do my own cooking, but I do not enjoy cleaning up. I do my own flowers and often my own invitations but am not capable of handling a bar at a large party. It is impossible to do it all!

How is your parking situation? Is one parker or two needed? These decisions will also determine the ease of which your party flows. Get as much help as you need or can afford. My young daughter loves to rinse herbs and separate the leaves for me. Her price is right, and she does a wonderful job. She is a big help with setting and clearing the table. Take help from whomever you can get it!

# Sonoma Supper with the Tommy Smothers Family

*The Smothers vineyard is one of the most beautiful places in California. Rows of precisely maintained vines are babied and coddled for the shear purpose of producing nectar that ferments into wine. In the center of this magnificence is an organic home built by Tommy, which incorporates many natural elements found on the property before one vine had been planted. Wood and stone abound in the inviting structure originally built as a bachelor pad for this funny man, but this pad has become a home for him, his wife, Marcy, their young son, Thomas Bolyn (i.e., Bo), and baby, Riley Rose, as well as Fenzel, the half golden lab/half golden retriever.*

Tommy and his family are very casual and have the art of entertaining down pat. Everyone in their home feels welcome and comfortable, and the foods they like are fresh and natural. In the Smothers household, the wine is as important as the food, and often the menu is based on the wine instead of vice versa. Spending time and cooking with the Smothers was a joy. They are warm, caring people surrounded by overwhelming beauty, and exceptional wine, food, and conversation were shared. The Smothers' Sonoma Supper was quite an introduction to the wine country experience!

*chef harry & friends*

*Sonoma Supper
with the Tommy
Smothers Family*

—— *hints* ——

- The Shrimp and Spinach Filo Spring Rolls can be assembled ahead and frozen up to ten days before baking.

- The grape leaf cigars, raspberry vinaigrette, chutney, and tart can be made up to thirty-six hours in advance.

- If time is a problem, purchase fresh Thai summer rolls at your favorite Thai restaurant and substitute for spring rolls.

- Buy a fruit tart for dessert.

- Make the vinaigrette the day before with the chutney.

- The lamb and olive sauté are quickly and easily prepared the day of the fun!

# m • e • n • u

Shrimp and Spinach Filo Spring Rolls

Sun Dried Tomatoes and Sonoma Goat Cheese Grape Leaf Cigars

Mixed Baby Greens and Asparagus with Raspberry Vinaigrette

Herb Marinated Sonoma Lamb Chops with Cranberry Mint Chutney

Grilled Torpedo Onions

Sauté of California Olives, Organic Fennel, and Rosemary

Raspberry Mascarpone Almond Tart

## Shrimp and Spinach Filo Spring Rolls

4 tablespoons unsalted butter

1½ tablespoons fresh finely chopped garlic

1 pound fresh shrimp, shelled and de-veined (we used
Tiger Shrimp)

8 ounces fresh baby spinach, washed and patted dry

salt and pepper to taste

1 box frozen filo pastry, thawed per directions

1/2 cup melted butter for filo pastry sheets

In a large, heavy, nonstick skillet over medium-high heat, heat butter and garlic and sauté until garlic turns golden brown. Stir in shrimp and sauté 2 minutes. Stir in spinach and sauté until wilted. Season with salt and pepper and remove from heat. When cool enough to proceed, coarsely chop mixture.

Unfold filo pastry and keep covered with damp towel. Place one piece on work surface and paint with melted butter. Fold in half lengthwise. Paint top with butter. Place a spoonful of the mixture at one end of the pastry. Roll end of pastry over filling and fold in both sides to contain filling and roll up like a small egg roll. Repeat to make 24 pieces. Place on buttered nonstick jelly roll pan and bake in preheated 350 degree oven until golden brown and crisp. They can be made the day before to point of baking, covered, and refrigerated until ready to bake.

Serves 8-12.

───── **hints** ─────
c o n t .

- "Zest" from any citrus refers to only the colored part of the rind. The white part is bitter. Scrape the zest with a tool designed just for the purpose of "zesting" or use a very sharp paring knife.

───── *words of* ─────
*a p p r e c i a t i o n*

*We are so very fortunate to be together and enjoy each other and the beauty and bounty set forth for our pleasures. We toast in appreciation of our beautiful lives!*

## Sun Dried Tomatoes and Sonoma Goat Cheese Grape Leaf Cigars

6 ounces fresh domestic goat cheese with herbs

6 ounces Sun Dried tomato puree (available in a gourmet department, or you can process drained marinated Sun Dried tomatoes in a food processor)

12 large grape leaves packed in brine

With a fork, mix together the goat cheese and Sun Dried tomato puree until a smooth paste is formed. Rinse the grape leaves thoroughly in water, and cut the leaves in half by removing the center spine of the leaf that runs into the stem. Pat dry. Spread the goat cheese paste over the leaf halves, and roll them up like cigars. They will stand upright on their cut end for serving. Cigars can be made a day in advance, covered, and refrigerated until ready to serve.

Makes 24 cigars.

## Mixed Baby Greens and Asparagus with Raspberry Vinaigrette

2/3 cup raspberry vinegar

2 tablespoons granulated sugar (or to taste)

4 minced shallots

1/4 cup rinsed fresh chopped basil leaves

rinsed fresh chopped oregano leaves to taste (just a sprig will do)

1/2 cup extra virgin olive oil

salt and pepper to taste

2 cups fresh raspberries

2 bunches blanched fresh baby asparagus, trimmed and cut into
    bite-sized pieces

12 ounces fresh mixed salad greens, rinsed and spun dry

Whisk together all dressing ingredients except oil. Continue to whisk, and add olive oil in a stream. Add oil slowly enough, and whisk briskly enough, to cause a slight emulsification (thickening). Season with salt and pepper. (You can make this in a blender if you like.) Toss desired amount of vinaigrette with asparagus, greens, and raspberries.

Serves 8.

##  Cranberry Mint Chutney

24 ounces fresh cranberries          juice from one lime
1½ cups granulated sugar             1/2 cup rinsed fresh mint leaves
1 tsp. lime zest

Rinse cranberries in cold water and drain but do not dry. Place in heavy saucepan placed over medium-high heat. Stir in sugar, lime zest, and lime juice. Cook until contents begins to simmer, stirring occasionally. Reduce heat to keep mixture just simmering and gently simmer until cranberries are tender, about 12 minutes. Stir in mint leaves and simmer 2 minutes more. Remove from heat to heat-proof nonmetallic bowl, cover, and refrigerate up to 4 days. Serve at room temperature.

Makes about 2 pints.

*Sonoma Supper
with the Tommy
Smothers Family*

# Herb Marinated Sonoma Lamb Chops

2-3 lamb chops per person

*For one cup marinade (enough for 12 to 18 chops):*
1/4 cup soy sauce
2 tablespoons extra virgin olive oil
1/2 cup red wine
1 tablespoon fresh minced ginger
2 tablespoons fresh minced garlic

*For serving:*
1 cup rinsed fresh chopped herb leaves to taste (equal amounts of
    rosemary, basil, and thyme work great)

Marinate lamb chops up to 12 hours. Grill over medium-hot coals until done to preference. For well-done 1½-inch thick chops, about 5 minutes per side, 3 minutes per side for medium, and about 2 minutes per side for rare. Arrange lamb chops on platter and sprinkle liberally with minced fresh herbs to taste.

Garnish with grilled Torpedo onions or other purple onion.

Serves 4–6.

# Grilled Torpedo Onions

4 large fresh Torpedo or other purple onions
2 tablespoons extra virgin olive oil
1 tablespoon fresh minced garlic
salt and fresh cracked pepper to taste

---

*grilled*
*torpedo onions*

When up in Sonoma to interview the Smothers, I happened upon a farmer's market where a vendor was selling Torpedo onions (small purple onions shaped like torpedoes). I had to try them and found them very strong, firm, and delicious when grilled. Any purple onion will do in this case.

Split onions in half lengthwise, and remove any loose or unattractive outer layers. Place onions in a zipper lock bag with oil, garlic, salt, and pepper. Seal and gently shake bag to coat. Grill both sides over medium-hot coals until just tender, about 5 minutes per side.

Serves 4–6.

## Sauté of California Olives, Organic Fennel, and Rosemary

1 tablespoon extra virgin olive oil

1 tablespoon fresh minced garlic

24 to 36 ounces assorted drained stuffed olives of choice—select
   ones like almond stuffed, garlic stuffed, and jalapeno stuffed for
   an interesting blend

2 medium heads fennel, trimmed, cleaned, and sliced into
   thin strips

4 grilled Torpedo or purple onion halves, sliced as for stir fry

2 tablespoons rinsed fresh minced oregano or 2 teaspoons
   dried oregano

fresh cracked pepper to taste

Heat oil in a large, heavy sauté pan over medium-high heat and stir in garlic. Sauté garlic until golden and stir in olives and fennel. Sauté 3 to 5 minutes or until fennel is tender. Stir in grilled onion strips. Season with oregano and cracked pepper. Alt: Add fresh basil, rosemary, and/or other fresh herbs to taste.

Serves 6–8.

# Raspberry Mascarpone Almond Tart

2 cups ginger snaps

1 cup finely chopped pecans

1 1/2 sticks sweet butter,
  room temperature

1 teaspoon cinnamon

1 pound mascarpone cheese

1 1/2 cups sour cream

2 cups granulated sugar

1 tablespoon vanilla extract

3 tablespoons fresh lemon juice

5 eggs

1 1/2 tablespoons powdered sugar

4 to 5 pints fresh raspberries

2 cups apricot preserves

1 cup sliced almonds

In a food processor fitted with a steel blade, process the ginger snaps and pecans until crumbs are formed. Add chunks of butter to the bowl, with cinnamon. Pulse until mixed well and the texture of coarse meal is achieved. Divide crust between 2  12-inch false bottomed fluted side tart pans, and press filling in even layer over bottom and up sides of pans.

In the same bowl, process mascarpone, 1 cup of sour cream, granulated sugar, vanilla, and lemon juice until blended. Add eggs and pulse until combined smoothly.

Place foil under pans, and divide cheese filling between pans. Bake in preheated 325 degree ovens until tops of tarts dome up completely, about 60 to 70 minutes. Cool and chill in refrigerator.

Mix remaining 1/2 cup of sour cream with powdered sugar, and spread a thin layer over tops of tarts. Arrange raspberries artfully on top.

Melt apricot preserves in microwave until bubbly and paint over raspberries using a pastry brush. Press almonds around sides of tarts attractively. Chill until ready to serve

# Santa Fe Fete

*My wife's parents, Bernie and Marianne, had a home in Santa Fe, New Mexico, and we found it a great town in which to eat. Combining those culinary experiences with numerous trips to the Mansion on Turtle Creek in Dallas, Texas you will have the necessary influences for this menu. Placing lobster and goat cheese inside a tortilla is only the beginning of some of the luscious offerings from innovative Southwestern cuisine.*

I added some chips that are made in the style of those enjoyed at the Four Seasons Hotel in Beverly Hills. We had them with guacamole by the pool the first time my family visited Los Angeles to decide if we wanted to try and get Chef Harry on television. We moved to Malibu less than one year later to start shooting *Chef Harry & Friends* for public television. Now that's Hollywood!

chef harry & friends

*Santa Fe*
*Fete*

—— *hints* ——

- Make topping for nachos, the salsas, and the rice the day before.
- The rice can be reheated in the oven in a covered casserole dish and the nachos finished off just before the guests arrive.
- Tie your napkins with a piece of raffia and place a sombrero in the center of the table for a quick splash of the fiesta feeling.
- Turn over a straw cowboy hat, line with a napkin, and serve the chips in it!

# m • e • n • u

Artichoke Nachos

Salsa Las Virgenes

Salsa Diablo

Four Season Chips

Lobster and Goat Cheese Quesadillas

Texmati Rice with Pinons

Cinnamon Chocolate Strawberry Mousse

## Artichoke Nachos

1 cup marinated artichoke hearts, drained and chopped

1 cup yellow corn kernels, drained

1 cup sweet yellow or mild green pepper, diced

1 cup fresh scallions (including greens), minced

1 cup shredded Monterey Jack or Colby cheese

jalapeno slices to taste (optional)

1/2 cup fresh chopped cilantro leaves

1 cup mayonnaise (Not fat free but low fat is OK)

1 teaspoon Worcestershire sauce

1 tablespoon fresh minced garlic

1 large bag blue corn or other interesting tortilla chips

Mix together all ingredients except chips. Arrange chips in an even layer on an ovenproof platter or serving tray (you may use a nonstick jelly roll pan if presentation is not a factor). Spoon mixture over chips as evenly as possible and bake in a preheated 400 degree oven until topping is brown and bubbly, about 15 to 20 minutes. Serve hot, as is, or with sour cream, salsa, chopped tomato, black olives, and/or shredded lettuce.

Serves 8 as an appetizer.

## Salsa Las Virgenes

1 cup chopped mild fresh seeded
 green chile pepper

1 cup chopped seeded tomato

1/2 cup fresh minced cilantro

juice from 2 limes

1/2 cup chopped onion

salt and pepper to taste

—— *words of* ——
*appreciation*

*Before we partake in our Southwestern delights, we give thanks for our blessed lives and the beautiful world in which we live. We are influenced by people from all over the world and are enriched in many ways. The vast cultures of the world color our lives like the sunset sky, and we are so lucky to bask in the rainbow.*

Mix ingredients together and serve with tortilla chips. Can be made, placed in a covered jar, and refrigerated up to 2 days before serving.

Makes about 2 cups.

 ## Salsa Diablo

1/2 cup chopped jalapeno peppers

1/2 cup chopped mild fresh
   seeded green chile pepper

1/2 cup finely chopped tomatillos

2 tablespoons tequila (optional)

fresh chopped habanero peppers
   to taste (optional)

1 teaspoon ground cumin

1/2 cup seeded tomato

juice from 2 limes

1 teaspoon hot chili powder

salt and pepper to taste

Mix ingredients together and serve with tortilla chips. Can be made, placed in a covered jar, and refrigerated up to 2 days before serving.

Makes about 2 cups.

 ## Four Season Chips

8 small flour tortillas

safflower or canola oil for frying

salt for salting

Cut each tortilla into 8 triangles. (Stack them in a pile and cut in half with a sharp knife, cut those halves again, and then each quarter.) Fry in batches in hot oil until golden brown and crispy.

— *word of* —

*warning*

Always wear rubber gloves when cleaning or handling hot peppers! The juices and seeds can be dangerous!

Drain on paper towels and sprinkle with salt. Keep in warm oven (200 degrees) on paper towel lined tray until ready to serve.

Serves 8–12 as an appetizer.

## Lobster and Goat Cheese Quesadillas

2 cups cooked lobster meat (grilled or broiled is best for this recipe)
2 cups fresh crumbled herbed goat cheese or chévre (Not feta)
8 small flour tortillas
a small amount of oil for grilling the quesadillas

Divide the lobster and cheese among the tortillas, and fold tortillas over into half circles to cover filling. Brush a thin film of oil over a nonstick griddle or sauté pan over medium-high heat, and brown quesadillas on both sides to crisp tortillas and melt cheese, about 2 or 3 minutes per side. Hold finished quesadillas in warm oven while grilling the rest. Quesadillas can be cut in half to serve as appetizers or first courses.

Makes 8 quesadillas serving 8 as a first course or 4–6 as an entree.

## Texmati Rice with Pinons

1 tablespoon extra virgin olive oil
1 tablespoon fresh minced garlic
1 cup minced yellow or white onion
1 cup chopped bell pepper
1 cup pinons (pine nuts)

8 ounces Texmati rice
1 teaspoon salt or to taste
cracked pepper to taste
2 cups water or chicken or
   vegetable stock

In a large saucepan or small Dutch oven with tight fitting lid, heat the oil over medium-high heat and stir in the garlic and onion. Sauté until onion begins to brown. Stir in bell pepper and pinons and sauté 1 minute more. Stir in rice and sauté one last minute. Season with salt and pepper and stir in water or stock. Bring to boil, cover, and reduce heat to simmer. Simmer undisturbed until water is absorbed and rice is tender, about 25 minutes.

Serves 6–8.

# Cinnamon Chocolate Strawberry Mousse

| | |
|---|---|
| 1 quart heavy whipping cream | 2 quarts strawberries, |
| 3/4 cup powdered sugar | hulled and halved |
| 1/2 cup cocoa powder | 1/2 cup powdered sugar |
| 1 teaspoon cinnamon | 2 tablespoons brandy |
| 1/2 teaspoon vanilla extract | or cognac |

Place whipping cream in a chilled bowl and beat with electric beaters set on medium until cream begins to froth. Gradually add 3/4 cup sugar while beating, then cocoa powder, and lastly cinnamon. Beat until stiff peaks are formed, and add vanilla extract. Place in pastry bag with fluted tip or cover bowl with plastic wrap, refrigerate in either case. (If you do not have a pastry tube, you can just use dollops of the mousse for serving.)

Toss the strawberries with the 1/2 cup sugar and liqueur and divide among serving dishes. (Champagne glasses work great and are very dramatic. Pipe or spoon mousse on top and serve immediately.)

Serves 8–12.

# Lunch at Shambala with Tippi Hedron and Friends

*The scenic drive to Shambala is more like what I would have expected a drive in Africa to be like. The rustic southern California wild west countryside set me up for our audience of lions, tigers, elephants, leopards, and more. But Tippi, crop in hand, led me through the wilderness introducing me to some of the reasons why she created Shambala, this haven for abused wild animals that stands for animal rights world wide. Shambala is Tippi's life. She lives within it, and it lives within her.*

Throughout our lunch, we were observed by Shambala's inhabitants, and I felt for a moment what it must be like to be an animal watched by observers in a zoo. In particular, two elephants across the stream could not take their eyes off us. Luckily, I had prepared an elephant feast in addition to our vegetarian one. The elephants dined on fresh arugula and radicchio stuffed in whole wheat pitas and a dessert of hoards of assorted bananas.

The sweet little baby bananas almost caused a stampede!

## chef harry & friends

*Lunch at Shambala with Tippi Hedron and Friends*

—— *hints* ——

- With the exception of tossing the salad, this entire menu can be made a day in advance.

- The chocolate cake layers can be made two weeks in advance, wrapped tightly in plastic wrap, and frozen until ready to assemble cake.

- I find cleaning artichoke a real chore. Many gourmet markets and restaurants will sell them already poached and chilled. For more than six, I highly recommend letting your fingers do the walking!

# m • e • n • u

Curried Garbanzo Pate

Herbed Flatbreads

Peppered Garlic Aioli

Whole Poached Artichokes

Mixed Greens and Mango Tossed with Papaya Seed Vinaigrette

Chocolate Plantain Cake with Chocolate Mousse Frosting

## Curried Garbanzo Pate

31 ounces prepared garbanzo beans, drained

6 cloves fresh garlic

juice from 2 limes

2 pickled jalapeno peppers, stems removed, drained

1/2 cup toasted sesame seeds

1 tablespoon mild curry powder

8 ounces fat free plain yogurt

salt and pepper to taste

Place garbanzos, garlic, lime juice, jalapenos, sesame seeds, and curry in bowl of food processor fitted with steel blade. Process until contents are coarsely ground. Add yogurt and season with salt and pepper.

Makes about 3 cups of pate.

 ## Herbed Flatbreads

1 package (3 pieces) soft rectangular lavosh style flat bread or 6 large pitas, separated into 2 rounds each

1/8 cup extra virgin olive oil

1 tablespoon dried sweet basil

1 teaspoon dried oregano

salt and fresh cracked black pepper to taste

Unfold the flatbreads or arrange the pita tops and bottoms, with inside up. Brush lightly with olive oil and sprinkle with herbs, salt, and pepper. Bake on aluminum foil lined oven racks in 350

———— words of ————
appreciation

*In a world full of turmoil, the time we can be outside and one with nature are special and rare. We are blessed members of the wild kingdom and toast to those who reach out to make the lives of people and animals better and the world a more peaceful place.*

degree oven until breads begin to brown and crisp, about 15 minutes. Reduce oven heat to 200 degrees, and hold breads as they fully crisp, about 30 minutes more. Keep in warm oven until ready to serve. Can be made 2 or 3 days in advance and kept in an airtight container. You may warm them in the oven to recrisp if necessary.

Serves 8.

 ## Peppered Garlic Aioli

2 teaspoons fresh lemon juice

2 cloves fresh garlic

1 teaspoon sweet paprika

1 teaspoon fresh cracked pepper

1 teaspoon mild chili powder

8 ounces fat free yogurt

1 tablespoon fat free or low fat mayonnaise

Place all ingredients except yogurt and mayonnaise in bowl of food processor fitted with steel blade and pulse until pasty. Add yogurt and mayonnaise, pulsing to mix well.

Makes about 1 1/2 cups aioli, enough for 6–8 artichokes.

# Whole Poached Artichokes

6 large whole artichokes

3 lemons, cut in half

a large stock pot of boiling salted water

Rinse the artichokes. Take one, cut off about 1½ inches (about 1/4 of the artichoke) from the top with a sharp knife. Dig out the hairy choke from the center of the artichoke with a teaspoon, exposing the heart. Be sure to remove all of the "choke." Take one lemon half and squeeze over the artichoke, making sure a lot of the juice goes into the center over the heart (this keeps it from turning brown). Place the used half of the lemon in the boiling water. Repeat with remaining artichokes, and place all of them carefully into the boiling water with the lemon halves. Boil until center of artichoke feels tender when pierced with the tip of a sharp knife. Drain in a colander and cool under cold water to stop cooking. Wrap individually in plastic wrap and refrigerate until ready to use. To serve, arrange artichokes in the center of a serving plate and drizzle with aioli. Surround with salad tossed with mango and papaya seed vinaigrette.

Serves 6.

*chef harry & friends*

Lunch at
Shambala with
Tippi Hedron
and Friends

———— *t o a s t e d* ————
*t h r e a d   c o c o n u t*

Toast coconut by
placing dried
unsweetened coconut
(available at grocery
stores and health food
stores) in nonstick
sauté pan over medi-
um-high heat, stirring
often until coconut
begins to brown.
Remove from heat.

## Mixed Greens and Mango Tossed with Papaya Seed Vinaigrette

seeds from 1 papaya (eat the flesh for breakfast or use in fruit salad)

2 cloves fresh garlic

1 cup toasted thread coconut

1 tablespoon sugar

juice from 4 limes

1 cup shredded Parmesan cheese

1 cup extra virgin olive oil

salt to taste

2 cups chopped mango

assorted salad greens of choice

Place all ingredients except mango and greens in food processor or blender and process until combined well. Do not over process or texture will be lost. Toss with mango and greens.

Serves 8–10.

## Chocolate Plantain Cake with Chocolate Mousse Frosting

*For plantain chantilly cream:*

4 egg yolks

1 cup powdered sugar

1/4 cup unbleached all purpose flour

2 cups milk

1 teaspoon vanilla

2 very ripe plantains

1 cup heavy whipping cream

In a heavy saucepan over medium heat, whisk together the egg yolks, sugar, flour, and 1/2 cup of the milk until smooth. Gradually add the balance of the milk slowly while stirring constantly. Cook the mixture while stirring until contents begin to simmer. Simmer gently for 5 minutes, remove from heat, and stir in vanilla. Mash plantains quickly and stir into custard. Pour into glass heat-proof bowl, and cover with plastic wrap directly touching top of custard. Cool and refrigerate over night. Beat whipping cream until stiff and fold into custard just before assembling cake.

*For chocolate cake:*

1 cake mix or recipe of choice

Make 2 chocolate cakes in 8 to 10-inch rounds. Cool and remove from pans to rack. Slice both layers in 2 creating 4 rounds total.

*For chocolate mousse frosting:*

1 quart heavy whipping cream

1 cup powdered sugar

1/2 cup cocoa powder

Beat cold whipping cream in chilled bowl with chilled beaters on medium-high speed. Gradually add powdered sugar, then cocoa. Beat until stiff peaks are formed. Use immediately.

**Lunch at
Shambala with
Tippi Hedron
and Friends**

*To assemble cake:*

Divide Plantain Chantilly Cream between cake layers and frost with Chocolate Mousse Frosting. Refrigerate up to 24 hours before serving.

Serves 12.

# Festive Fall Celebration

*Growing up in Iowa where a lot of beef is raised, I often was presented a steak at dinner time. Iowa beef really spoiled me, and when we moved, I did not have too much beef because I did not want to be disappointed. Besides, I moved from Marshalltown, Iowa to Cambridge, Massachusetts. There was a whole new world of food out there. But every now and then, I get a craving for a steak. This menu is perfect for a crisp fall evening. It takes me right back to the farm!*

*chef harry & friends*

*Festive Fall
Celebration*

- The Garlic Crostini can be made a day or two in advance and crisped in a warm oven.

- Prepare all the ingredients for the Popcorn Shrimp Bruschetta in the morning, then give a quick toss just before assembling.

- You can make the bacon dressing hours ahead of time and just reheat it before adding the cheese.

- The Peach Crumble can be made the morning and warmed in the oven before serving.

- You may pre-grill the mushrooms, they will have a smoky flavor and just take a minute to sauté.

# m • e • n • u

Popcorn Shrimp Bruschetta with
Garlic Crostini

Bacon Gorgonzola Spinach

Sautéed Mushrooms

Grilled New York Strip Steak

Peach Crumble

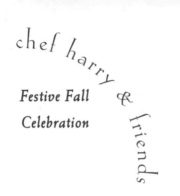

 Garlic Crostini

1 stick butter or 1/4 cup extra virgin olive oil

1/8 cup fresh minced garlic

1 day old baguette, sliced into 24 to 30 slices about 2/3 inch thick

Heat the butter or oil with the garlic until the garlic begins to toast a bit. Brush one side of each slice of bread with mixture and sauté in batches in nonstick, heavy sauté pan or griddle over medium heat until browned, about 4 minutes per side. Hold in 200 degree oven and crisp overnight.

Serves 6–8

hints
cont.

- Many people do not eat meat. Make plenty of bruschetta, spinach, and mushrooms, and they will still be happy campers!

 Popcorn Shrimp Bruschetta

4 firm tomatoes, seeded and chopped

2 tablespoons fresh minced garlic

3 tablespoons extra virgin olive oil

1 teaspoon red wine or balsamic vinegar

salt and pepper to taste

1/2 pound cooked popcorn (baby) shrimp or chopped large
cocktail shrimp

24 to 30 Garlic Crostini, warm

Toss together all ingredients except crostini. Divide mixture among crostini and serve.

Any leftover can be tossed with some greens for a wonderful salad the next day. Save a couple of crostini, break them up for croutons, and voila! Lunch is ready!

Serves 6–8.

*words of*
*appreciation*

*Fall harvest is a time to appreciate the bounty we are so lucky to enjoy. As we gather together around the table to share all that is delivered from this earth, let us give thanks for life's blessings.*

 Bacon Gorgonzola Spinach

1 pound lean bacon, chopped

1 tablespoon fresh minced garlic

1 cup pine nuts, walnut pieces, or pecan halves (optional,
   but great)

1 teaspoon or more fresh cracked pepper

2 tablespoons sugar

1/2 cup rinsed fresh chopped basil leaves

2/3 cup red wine vinegar

1 cup crumbled Gorgonzola cheese

12-16 ounces fresh rinsed baby spinach leaves

In a deep, heavy sauté pan over medium-high heat, cook bacon with garlic until browned and crisp. Do not drain! Turn off heat and stir in nuts, pepper, sugar, basil, and vinegar. Now quickly stir in cheese and toss in spinach. Serve immediately.

Serves 6 as a salad and 8 as a side dish.

 Sautéed Mushrooms

1 to 1½ pounds mushrooms of choice—oyster mushrooms and
   portobellos are great with beef

1/8 cup extra virgin olive oil (optional)

1 tablespoon fresh minced garlic

1 stick butter

2 tablespoons good drinking sherry

1/2 teaspoon Worcestershire sauce

salt and pepper to taste

Rinse and pick over the mushrooms. Drain them on paper towel. There is now room for an optional step: If desired, combine the olive oil with the garlic and brush over the mushrooms. Place on hot grill for 30 seconds per side, remove to plate and refrigerate until ready to sauté. (If you do not pre-grill, heat the garlic with the butter before sautéing mushrooms.) Heat butter (and garlic if not used for grilling) in heavy, nonstick sauté pan over medium-high heat, and sauté mushrooms until hot and tender, about 2 to 5 minutes. Stir in sherry. Season with Worcestershire sauce, salt, and pepper. Serve immediately.

Serves 6–8.

# Grilled New York Strip Steak

*Marinade for 6–8 steaks:*
3 tablespoons extra virgin olive oil
2 tablespoons fresh minced garlic
1/4 cup soy sauce
2 tablespoons fresh cracked pepper

Toss steaks with marinade and refrigerate up to 24 hours. Bring steaks to room temperature and grill over medium-hot coals, turning once until desired doneness is reached; about 2 minutes per side for rare, 4 minutes per side for medium, and 5½ minutes per side for well-done.

Serves 6–8.

# Peach Crumble

*For the peach filling:*

8-10 firm but ripe peaches, pitted and sliced

1 cup powdered sugar

1/4 cup unbleached all purpose flour

1 teaspoon vanilla extract

*For the topping:*

1 stick cold butter, cut into chunks

1 cup brown sugar

1/2 cup granulated sugar

1 cup oatmeal

1 cup unbleached all purpose flour

1 teaspoon cinnamon

Place topping ingredients in food processor and pulse until the texture of coarse meal. Toss the peach slices with powdered sugar, 1/4 cup flour, and vanilla. Turn peaches into deep buttered 10 x 12-inch baking dish and cover with topping in an even layer. Bake in preheated 350 degree oven until bubbly and topping is browned and crisp, about 35 to 40 minutes.

Serves 8–12.

# Centered Cuisine with Deepak Chopra

*Visiting the Deepak Chopra Center for Well Being in La Jolla is an experience. Just walking through the door, it is impossible not to sense the calm, the peace, and the harmony. The colors, the surfaces, and the architecture are all perfect. One is immediately comfortable and soothed. After meeting Deepak, it was obvious why. He is a charming man with an aura of wisdom. During our time together, he was frequently interrupted by faxes from all over the world. He never lost focus. He is steadfast in his views of the relationship between spiritual and physical well being and what we eat. He is indeed inspiring.*

The charming, hands-on, executive chef, Ginna Bell Bragg, is a kindred spirit. We liked each other immediately and felt the same about the importance of love in the kitchen and the balance of spices and content in what we prepare. Her cuisine, all vegetarian, is creative and delicious. We could have played all day! The recipes that follow are my versions of her creations. Yes, she inspired me, too!

*chef harry & friends*

Centered
Cuisine with
Deepak Chopra

—— *hints* ——

- The Vegetable Strudel can be assembled a day in advance, refrigerated, and then baked just before serving.

- The rice may be made a day ahead of time, as may the dressing. They can be combined just before serving.

- Bake the French Apple Cake early in the morning and rewarm to serve.

- The Morning Chai can become habitual.

# m · e · n · u

Vegetable Strudel

Wild Rice Salad

French Apple Cake

Morning Chai

# Vegetable Strudel

5 cups mixed vegetables (a good recipe to clean out the bin-use
  potatoes, carrots, onions, peppers, squash), trimmed and
  chopped into bite sized pieces

1 tablespoon butter or ghee or olive oil

8 ounces corn kernels, frozen or canned, drained

8 ounces peas, frozen or canned, drained

1/2 cup fresh chopped basil leaves

1 teaspoon dried oregano

1/2 teaspoon fresh minced rosemary leaves

soy sauce to taste, about 1 tablespoon

fresh cracked pepper to taste

1 box filo pastry sheets, thawed according to directions

1/4 cup melted butter

sesame seeds for sprinkling (optional)


In a large, nonstick heavy skillet over medium-high heat, sauté
the vegetables in the 1 tablespoon butter or oil until tender. Stir
in herbs and season with soy sauce and pepper. Cool.

Unfold a sheet of filo and paint with melted butter. Top with
another sheet, paint, and repeat, using 6 sheets of pastry on top of
each other. Place the layered filo on a buttered rectangular baking
dish or jelly roll pan. Place the vegetable filling in a line down the
center and enclose with the sides and ends of the pastry like a
giant burrito. Paint with melted better and bake in preheated 375
degree oven until pastry is brown and flaky, about 30 minutes.

Serves 6–8.

chef harry &
friends

Centered
Cuisine with
Deepak Chopra

—— words of ——
appreciation

*The spirit within us rises when
it is nurtured. Food for the
body is food for the soul.
May we sense the peace
amidst the chaos around us
and let it reflect from our
hearts as we give thanks for
the gift of life.*

 Wild Rice Salad

3 cups cooked wild rice or blend, cooled

1 tablespoon olive oil

1 cup fresh diced fennel bulb

1 cup chopped seeded yellow or red tomato

1/4 cup pine nuts

1/4 cup fresh dill

1/2 cup chopped scallion

1/4 cup lime juice

juice from one lemon

1 tablespoon sugar or honey

salt and pepper to taste

Toss the rice with the olive oil and stir in fennel, tomato, pine nuts, dill, and scallions. Mix together the lime and lemon juice, sugar, salt, and pepper. Toss with rice mixture and serve, or cover and refrigerate up to 24 hours. Serve room temperature.

Serves 4–6.

 French Apple Cake

*For the cake:*

2 pounds tart apples, chopped

1/2 teaspoon ground cinnamon

1/2 teaspoon ground clove

2 cups unbleached all purpose flour

2 teaspoons baking powder

1/2 cup granulated sugar

1 tablespoon maple syrup

1/2 cup milk

1/4 cup melted butter

4 eggs plus 2 egg whites, slightly beaten

*For the topping:*

2 eggs, slightly beaten

1/4 cup melted butter

1 cup light brown sugar

1 tablespoon almond extract

1/4 cup sliced almonds

Toss the apples with the cinnamon and clove and pour into a buttered 9 x 12-inch baking dish or cake pan. Mix together the flour, baking powder, and sugar. Stir in the syrup, milk, butter, and eggs and beat 90 seconds. Pour over apples and bake in pre-heated 325 degree oven until golden brown, about 45 minutes.

Mix together topping ingredients except almonds and pour over cake just as it comes out of the oven. Sprinkle almonds over topping, and return cake to oven for about 20 minutes. Topping should be brown and bubbly.

Serves 8–10.

*Centered*
*Cuisine with*
*Deepak Chopra*

 Morning Chai

4 cups water

2 English Breakfast type tea bags

1/4 teaspoon cinnamon

seeds from 1 papaya (optional, but really makes it great)

1/4 teaspoon ginger root powder

1/4 cup milk

honey to taste

Bring the water to a boil. Remove from heat, and add tea, cinnamon, papaya seeds, and ginger. Allow to stand for 7 minutes and stir in milk and honey.

Makes 4 cups.

# Low Country Style Eats

*When touring to introduce my first book,* Easygoing Entertaining, *I found Charleston, South Carolina to be a most warm and inviting place. The food is incredible, the people are charming, and the city is one of the most beautiful on the East Coast. Being a runner, I love to wake in Charleston, don my running shoes, and work up my appetite between Battery Park and Charleston Bay.*

Anyway, I was to be interviewed by the food editor for the Charleston paper, and she asked me to come to her office, which was unusual. When I arrived, she greeted me with several bags of groceries and a heavy cooler. She said, "grab what you can, we are going for a ride!"

Over to Johnson and Wales Cooking School's kitchen we went, and after unloading (it was quite a walk with our load of groceries, and I was exhausted by the time we got to the kitchen), she looked at me and said, "Using only the ingredients we have here, prepare me a four course 'Low Country' meal. You have three hours." Yeah, right. First of all, what the heck does "Low Country" mean? I had not a clue but could not expose that to the woman who was going to plaster me holding my new book on the front page of an up and coming food section in the paper.

I figured that she must be expecting something regional; something "Suuuuuthern;" something spicy. Before me, I found shrimp, rice, okra, grits, corn on the cob, squash, onions, peppers, garlic, and apples along with many essentials like butter, oil, cream, flour, eggs, etc. I had to choose between going back to the hotel and forgetting about ever promoting my book again or hunting for a knife, pan, and cutting board in this strange institutional kitchen. I looked at her and asked, "Are you going to tie one hand behind my back before I start?"

I began by separating what might go into a dessert, which I thought I should start with since it might take the longest to finish if baking was to be involved. Next, the entree ingredient choices, and finally, the side dishes. I may have, up to that point and slightly beyond, looked like I knew what I was doing.

I was paring some apples and putting together an apple cobbler in my mind while looking around the room for things like a mixing bowl, a baking dish, and an oven; little things that could come in handy. After a few minutes, my cobbler was ready to put in the oven, and I could tell she was impressed. I began to relax as I turned my back on the oven door I had just closed.

Moving on to the other dishes, I was starting to have fun. About thirty minutes later, I smelled smoke...a very bad sign unless you are outside at the grill. I flung the oven door open to see a charred apple cobbler. Not yet panicking, I searched for a hot pad, grabbed a towel, and took this disaster out of the oven. Seems I had picked the oven that had a calibration problem. It had two settings: off and 500 degrees. No one bothered to let me know that bit of information. I looked into the food editor's eyes as I held my cremated cobbler and felt like my clothes had just jumped off my body. I had been exposed in the kitchen!

I gathered my (positive) thoughts, quickly scraped all the burned stuff off my sad looking cobbler, and tasted the apples. Thankfully, they did not taste burned. I turned them into a buttered loaf pan, covered them with cream, grated some lemon rind over the top, and put it back into a 350 degree oven, which I was assured worked properly. The result was a fabulous Apple Lemon Loaf that proved to be the hit of the meal—proof positive that I have a guardian angel for which I am most appreciative!

# chef harry & friends

*Low Country
Style Eats*

# m • e • n • u

Fried Okra

Garlic Peppered Dipping Sauce

Grilled Yellow Squash

Cheese Grits with Fresh Corn and
Green Chilies

Peppered Shrimp

Apple Lemon Loaf

## ——— hints ———

- Make the dipping
  sauce and Apple Lemon
  Loaf the day ahead, and
  warm the apple loaf
  before serving.
- You may pre-grill the
  squash up to one day
  in advance and sauté
  quickly before serving
  or serve room
  temperature.

 ## Fried Okra

1 cup unbleached all purpose flour

1 tablespoon fresh cracked pepper

1 pound fresh okra, trimmed and rinsed

4 eggs, beaten until slightly frothy

canola or safflower oil for frying

kosher salt for sprinkling over fried okra

Sprinkle a little flour over a nonstick tray or large piece of waxed paper. Combine the rest of the flour with the pepper, and toss the mixture in a sealed large zipper lock bag with the okra. Shake to dust each piece. Remove the okra from the bag, and place the balance of the peppered flour on a dinner plate. Dip each piece of okra in egg and again in the flour and place on floured tray or paper. Deep fry in batches in hot oil until golden brown, removing to paper towel lined heat-proof tray. Hold in 200 degree oven. When all okra is fried, sprinkle with salt to taste and serve.

Serves 8 as an appetizer.

## Garlic Peppered Dipping Sauce

3/4 cup mayonnaise

juice from 1 lemon

1 tablespoon fresh cracked pepper

1/2 teaspoon paprika

1 tablespoon fresh minced garlic

—— words of ——
appreciation

*North, South, East, and West, we do not have to travel far to know how fortunate we are. Being together and enjoying Low Country cuisine brings high country spirits. We give thanks for life's beauty in every direction.*

dash of Worcestershire sauce

hot pepper sauce to taste (i.e., Tabasco, etc.)

Blend together all ingredients, cover, and refrigerate until ready to serve. Can be made up to 2 days in advance.

Makes about 1 cup.

 ## Grilled Yellow Squash

4 yellow squash

2 tablespoons extra virgin olive oil

1 teaspoon fresh minced garlic

salt and pepper to taste

Slice squash into 1/2-inch slices and toss with oil, garlic, salt, and pepper. Grill over medium-hot coals until tender, about 90 seconds per side. Serve hot or warm. You may also slice the squash into strips at this point and sauté quickly in butter before serving.

Serves 6–8.

 ## Cheese Grits with Fresh Corn and Green Chilies

1/2 cup unsalted butter

1 tablespoon fresh minced garlic

1 cup chopped white or yellow onion

1 cup chopped sweet green chile

1 cup coarse grits

2 to 3 cups milk

1 cup fresh corn kernels

1 cup cheddar cheese, shredded

salt and pepper to taste

Heat the butter in a heavy saucepan over medium-high heat and stir in garlic and onion. Sauté until onion begins to turn golden. Stir in green chilies and grits and sauté 1 minute. Reduce heat to medium. Slowly stir in 2 cups of the milk and continue stirring until contents begin to simmer. Reduce heat to low and simmer, stirring occasionally, for 25 to 30 minutes. Contents should be thick. Add more milk as needed to make smooth and stir in corn and cheese. Stir until cheese melts, adding more milk if needed.

Serves 6–8 as a side dish or 4–6 for breakfast.

 ## Peppered Shrimp

1 stick unsalted butter

2 tablespoons vegetable or olive oil

1 tablespoon fresh minced garlic

1 cup chopped white or yellow onion

1 cup chopped celery

1 cup fresh asparagus, trimmed and cut into bite-sized pieces

2 pounds fresh shrimp, cleaned and rinsed

salt, cayenne pepper, and crushed red pepper to taste

Heat butter, oil, garlic, and onion in large, heavy, nonstick sauté pan over medium-high heat and sauté until onion begins to turn golden. Stir in celery and asparagus and sauté 2 minutes. Stir in shrimp and sauté until almost done. Season with salt and peppers and serve immediately.

Serves 6–8.

# Apple Lemon Loaf

5 large apples, peeled, cored, and thinly sliced

1/4 cup unbleached all purpose flour

1 cup granulated or powdered sugar

1 teaspoon cinnamon

zest from 2 lemons

juice from 2 lemons

1 cup heavy cream

Toss all ingredients together except cream and press into buttered loaf pan to accommodate. Cover with foil and bake in preheated 350 degree oven for 60 minutes. Remove from oven, uncover, and pour cream over top. Return to oven uncovered and bake 15 to 20 minutes more, until top begins to brown. Remove from oven and let sit for 10 minutes. Serve over ice cream.

Serves 8.

# Picnic on the Beach with JoBeth Williams and Family

*We moved to Malibu a couple of months before JoBeth and her family rented a beach house about four doors down from ours. We were having one of our first beach buffets for the neighbors, and a few other new friends and JoBeth wandered down. Charming and warm, we were all taken by her down to earth nature, and we instantly hit it off, as I love to cook and she loves to eat!*

When I asked her if I could come into their beach house for my television show and invade their vacation, she was thrilled to have a party in her home where she did not have to worry about a thing. We all had a great time. One nice thing about Malibu is that you never know who is going to wander down the beach!

*Picnic on the
Beach with
JoBeth Williams
and Family*

--- h i n t s ---

- Freeze the vodka up to ten days in advance.
- The shrimp can be pre-grilled the day before (while grilling chicken for dinner perhaps) and quickly reheated just prior to serving.
- Make the potatoes, and corn pepper relish the day before and toss with greens just before serving.
- The crumble can be made early in the day and reheated prior to serving.
- The chicken can be made an hour or two in advance and held in a warm oven.

# m • e • n • u

Cranberry Coolers

Glacier Vodka

Grilled Shrimp Tandoori Style

New Potatoes with Dilled Shallot Vinaigrette

Corn Pepper Relish and Greens

Garlic Crusted Fried Chicken

Raspberry Blueberry Crumble `a la Mode

##  Cranberry Coolers

1 pound each red and green seedless grapes

32 ounces cranberry cocktail

1 bottle chilled champagne (alcoholic or non)

Remove grapes from skeleton, arrange in a single layer on a tray, and freeze. When frozen, you may place them in a plastic bag and keep frozen until ready to use. Place 6 or 8 grapes in a champagne glass, fill half with cranberry cocktail, and top with champagne. The grapes will be the best part!

Makes 8–12 drinks.

##  Glacier Vodka

1 lemon

1 750-ml bottle vodka (Gin works well, too. I pick something in a blue bottle for appearance.)

1 empty and rinsed 1/2 gallon milk carton

a few flowers and some greenery

Using a strip peeler or knife, remove strips of lemon rind and cut into 1/2-inch lengths. Place in bottle of vodka, and recap bottle. Set bottle inside milk carton and fill with water until 2 inches from top of carton. Arrange flowers and greenery attractively around bottle making sure all decoration is submerged in water. Freeze until solid. To unmold, peel off carton, and run block under cold water. Wrap with towel to serve and place in a dish lined with a cloth napkin to catch the water as the ice melts.

*chef harry & friends*

Picnic on the
Beach with
JoBeth Williams
and Family

—— *words of* ——
*a p p r e c i a t i o n*

*The crashing surf, the
lavender-blue sky and the
laughter of children all
remind us of the happiness
that fills the earth. When
the water meets the sand
it is announced, sometimes
with a whisper and
sometimes with a crash.
May our words, no matter
how loudly spoken, always
land on ears like whispers.*

## Grilled Shrimp Tandoori Style

2 pounds cleaned large shrimp

1 tablespoon mild curry powder

1 tablespoon sweet paprika

3 tablespoons fresh minced garlic

juice from 4 limes

1 tablespoon soy sauce

2 tablespoons sesame oil

2 tablespoons ground cumin

Toss shrimp with remainder of ingredients and skewer for grilling or broiling. Grill over medium-hot coals until just cooked, about 2 minutes per side. Serve hot or cold with Peppered Peanut Dipping Sauce, (p. 82).

Serves 8–12.

 ## New Potatoes with Dilled Shallot Vinaigrette

5 pounds new potatoes, as uniform in size as possible, scrubbed

salted water for boiling potatoes

1/2 cup extra virgin olive oil

1/2 cup red wine vinegar

2 tablespoons granulated sugar (or to taste)

1 teaspoon dried oregano

1/2 cup fresh chopped basil

salt and pepper to taste

1 tablespoon Dijon mustard

1/2 cup minced dill weed

1 cup chopped red onion

Poach potatoes in salted boiling water until just tender when speared with a knife. Rinse gently under cold water. Mix together oil, vinegar, sugar, oregano, basil, salt, pepper, mustard, and dill. Toss gently with potatoes and onion. Place into oiled glass bowl that just barely accommodates the mixture and press in. Cover with plastic wrap, and place a plate on top and a heavy can or pan on top of that. Refrigerate overnight and unmold onto serving platter to serve.

Serves 8.

## Corn Pepper Relish and Greens

1 pound frozen corn kernels, thawed and rinsed

4 multi-color bell peppers, sliced thinly into strips

1½ tablespoons ground cumin

1 teaspoon sweet chili powder

1 minced red onion

juice from 4 limes

salt and pepper to taste

a pinch of sugar (optional)

8 ounces mixed fresh greens

Toss all ingredients except greens together, cover, refrigerate, and allow to marinate a couple hours or overnight. Before serving, toss with greens or serve atop greens as desired.

Serves 6–8.

 ## Garlic Crusted Fried Chicken

4 skinless boneless chicken breasts, split into 8 pieces total

4 eggs, lightly beaten

2 cups bread crumbs

1 tablespoon dried oregano

2 tablespoons dried basil

2 tablespoons salt

1 tablespoon fresh cracked pepper

1/8 cup fresh minced garlic

canola or safflower oil for frying

Rinse the chicken in water and place in a bowl with eggs. Toss to coat and allow to sit for 10 minutes. Meanwhile, mix the bread-crumbs with the oregano, basil, salt, and pepper. Dredge chicken in bread crumbs to coat.

Heat 1/4-inch layer oil in a heavy, nonstick sauté pan over medium-high heat and stir in 1/2 of the minced garlic. Fry four pieces of the chicken, turning once until golden brown and juice runs clear when chicken is pierced with the tip of a knife. (Do that after removing from pan or juice will cause hot oil to splatter and you could get burned.Ouch!) Drain on paper towels and hold in warm oven while repeating with other batch. It is not necessary to change oil between batches. Just add oil to replace what was used with first batch and stir in balance of garlic.

Makes 8 pieces.

# Raspberry Blueberry Crumble à la Mode

*For the berries:*
2 pints fresh raspberries
2 pints fresh blueberries
1 cup powdered sugar
1/4 cup unbleached all purpose flour

*For the topping:*
1 stick butter cut into pieces
1 cup oatmeal
1 cup unbleached flour
2 cups brown sugar
1 cup granulated sugar
1 teaspoon cinnamon

Toss berries with powdered sugar and 1/4 cup flour. Place in buttered deep 8x10 baking dish. Pulse topping ingredients until the texture of coarse meal in food processor. Place in even layer covering berries. Bake in preheated 350 degree oven until bubbly and brown on top, about 50 minutes.

Serves 8 or up to 12 served à la Mode.

# A Healthful Holiday Breakfast

*The perfect Christmas or New Year's breakfast, or any day of the year you want to start out right. With but a small amount of canola oil for the potatoes and a touch of butter to keep the pancakes from sticking to the pan, this menu is virtually fat free. My wife has me make the pancakes when she gets hungry for pumpkin pie—about twice a month!*

*A Healthful
Holiday
Breakfast*

——— *hints* ———

- The chutney and the Rosemary Roasted Potatoes can be made the day before and warmed before serving.

- Freeze champagne flutes for the Berry Yogurt Velvet. Wedge a strawberry on the glass when serving, or garnish with a sprig of fresh mint.

# m · e · n · u

Berry Yogurt Velvet

Spiced Pumpkin Pancakes

Warm Apple Cinnamon Chutney

Rosemary Roasted Potatoes

Hot Chocolate

# Berry Yogurt Velvet

12 ounces fat free raspberry yogurt

2 ripe bananas

1 cup fresh strawberries

1 teaspoon vanilla extract

1 tablespoon honey

mint leaves for garnish

Place ingredients except mint in blender and blend until smooth. Serve in dramatic glasses or champagne flutes. You may also serve in frozen margarita glasses. Garnish with mint sprigs.

Serves 2–3.

 # Spiced Pumpkin Pancakes

1 cup puree of pumpkin flesh, either canned or fresh roasted

1 cup unbleached all purpose flour

1 teaspoon baking powder

1 teaspoon ground cinnamon

1/2 teaspoon ground clove

1 cup granulated sugar

1/2 teaspoon vanilla extract

4 large egg whites

1 tablespoon of butter for frying pancakes

Mix together pumpkin, flour, baking powder, cinnamon, clove, sugar, and vanilla until well blended. Mix egg whites into mixture and stir well.

A Healthful
Holiday
Breakfast

——— *words of* ———
*appreciation*

*We start this day, as always, being thankful for our beautiful lives and happiness. May we be lucky enough to touch a life with kindness today and bring a smile to the face of another.*

Heat a large, heavy, nonstick skillet over medium-high heat and swirl around just enough butter to season the pan. Spoon pools of batter into 4-inch circles, and reduce heat to medium, cooking pancakes about 2 minutes before turning when beginning to brown.

Cook 2 to 3 minutes more. Remove to warm platter and hold in oven until all pancakes are ready to be served. Serve immediately.

Makes about 12 pancakes.

 ## Warm Apple Cinnamon Chutney

4-6 cored apples, chopped
1/4 to 1/2 cup sugar (depending on tartness of apples)
1 teaspoon ground cinnamon
juice from 1 lime

Mix ingredients in heavy saucepan over medium heat and bring to simmer. Reduce heat and simmer 10 minutes. Remove to heat-proof glass or ceramic bowl and cool. Cover and refrigerate until ready to serve. Can be made up to 3 days in advance.

Makes about 2 cups.

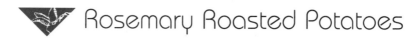 ## Rosemary Roasted Potatoes

6 medium baking potatoes, scrubbed clean
2 tablespoons olive oil
1/2 cup fresh minced red bell pepper

1/2 cup minced red onion

1 tablespoon fresh minced garlic

1/4 cup fresh rosemary leaves, chopped coarsely

kosher salt and fresh cracked pepper to taste

Toss all ingredients together and arrange in a layer on an oiled jelly roll pan. Roast in 325 degree oven until brown and tender, about 90 minutes to 2 hours.

Serves 6–8.

## Hot Chocolate

*For each serving:*

1 tablespoon cocoa powder

2 tablespoons sugar

2 tablespoons water

1 cup skim milk

a drop or 2 of vanilla extract

marshmallows for garnish

Stir cocoa, sugar, and water in a heavy saucepan over medium heat until it begins to simmer. Slowly stir in milk and when hot, add vanilla. Serve hot with marshmallows if desired.

# Low Fat Southwestern for Geraldo Rivera

*After talking for the first time to Geraldo's wife, C. C., I knew I was going to have fun at the sprawling waterside estate in New Jersey. As we finished talking the last time before I was to leave to meet them, she said, "Oh, and Harry, Geraldo will take care of the Margaritas." That sounded great to me, even though I rarely consume any alcohol. I am always up for a specialty of the house.*

I had a ball with the Riveras. They made me feel like one of the group from the beginning. Their house is full of activity from squawking birds and barking dogs to laughing children and ringing phones. By the end of the evening, having melted a couple of margaritas from the Rivera Frozen Monster Margarita Maker down my thirsty throat (we celebrity chefs work hard, you know!), I had the opportunity to sit across the table and learn first hand exactly why Geraldo is one of the most successful men on television. He is a genius, very generous, quick witted and backed up by one great woman.

*Low Fat
Southwestern
for Geraldo
Rivera*

— *hints* —

- The Cilantro Pickled Shellfish, coulis, tortilla chips, Corn Cumin Relish, tamale bake, pinto beans, Pico de Gallo, and Cinnamon Meringues with Fresh Strawberry Sauce can all be made a day in advance.

- You could leave out the shellfish, sole, and pinto beans and still have a banquet!

# m • e • n • u

## Cilantro Pickled Shellfish

## Roasted Garlic and Cubanelle Pepper Coulis

## Baked Tortilla Chips

## Chili Blackened Sole over Corn Cumin Relish

## Yellow Tomato and Jicama Salad with Toasted Pepitas

## Chicken Tamale Bake with Jalapeno Smashed Potatoes

## Pinto Beans with Plantains and Cilantro

## Pico de Gallo

## Cinnamon Meringues with Fresh Strawberry Sauce

# Cilantro Pickled Shellfish

juice from 6 fresh limes with enough water for 1 1/2 cups

1/2 cup granulated sugar

1 teaspoon salt

1 cup fresh chopped cilantro

1 minced fresh seeded jalapeno pepper (Wear rubber gloves when
   handling hot peppers.)

1 pound cooked cleaned cocktail shrimp

1 pound cooked lobster tail meat, cut into chunks

1 pound fresh cooked squid rings or bay scallops

Toss all ingredients together. Cover and refrigerate up to 36 hours.

Serves 8.

# Roasted Garlic and Cubanelle Pepper Coulis

4 large heads elephant garlic or 8 heads regular garlic, cleaned and
   separated into cloves

6 sweet green peppers (cubanelles) cleaned and split in
   half lengthwise

2 tablespoons extra virgin olive oil

salt and pepper to taste

Place garlic and peppers in shallow roasting pan and toss with
oil. Sprinkle with salt and pepper. Roast in 325 degree oven
until garlic is soft and browned, about 1 hour. Cool and scrape

——— *words of* ———
*appreciation*

*In life there are many
obstacles. How we overcome
them is what determines the
pattern of our lives. How
fortunate we are to be able to
share strength with one
another by being here together.
To life!*

pan contents into bowl of food processor fitted with steel blade. Process until smooth. Serve room temperature.

Makes about 1¼ cup.

 ## Baked Tortilla Chips

1 package blue corn tortillas (available at health food stores)
1 tablespoon olive oil
salt for sprinkling

Brush tortillas with oil and stack. With sharp knife, cut tortillas in half, cut those halves into halves, and those halves into halves again. Arrange on cookie sheets in single layer and sprinkle with salt. Bake in preheated 325 degree oven until browned, turn off heat, and leave in oven until crisp.

Serves 6–8.

 ## Chili Blackened Sole

5 fresh sole filets, cut in halves for 10 pieces
1/4 cup mild to hot chili powder (depending on taste)
1/4 cup ground cumin
1/3 cup sweet paprika
2 limes

Mix together the paprika, chili powder, and cumin. Rinse fish and dredge in spice mixture to coat thoroughly.

Heat a large, heavy, nonstick skillet over high heat until very hot. Carefully arrange 1/2 of the fish pieces in the pan leaving room between pieces to facilitate turning. Cook about 90 seconds on one side (it should begin to have black spots on the cooked side) and carefully turn. Cook another minute until fish is just done (white through and through). Squeeze the juice from 1 lime over the fish and remove to warm platter. Hold in oven until other half of fish pieces are complete, squeezing lime juice over each batch as with the first. Serve with Corn Cumin Relish.

Serves 5–8.

 ## Corn Cumin Relish

1 cup chopped pimento stuffed olives

2 cups frozen sweet corn kernels, rinsed and thawed

2 tablespoons ground cumin

1 tablespoon mild chili powder

juice from 2 limes

a pinch of sugar if desired

Toss ingredients together. Cover and refrigerate up to 24 hours before serving.

Serves 5–8.

# Yellow Tomato and Jicama Salad with Toasted Pepitas

1 cup pepitas (pine nuts will work if you have no source for pepitas)

1 tablespoon fresh minced garlic

2/3 cup red wine vinegar

1/8 cup granulated sugar

1/2 cup safflower oil

1/2 cup fresh chopped cilantro

1/2 cup fresh chopped basil leaves

salt and freshly cracked pepper to taste

4 firm yellow tomatoes, trimmed, washed, and sliced

2 medium jicama, peeled and cut into attractive pieces for salad

In a nonstick sauté pan over medium heat, sauté the pepitas until toasted. Remove from heat. Mix together the garlic, vinegar, sugar, oil, cilantro, garlic, salt, and pepper. Arrange the tomato and jicama on platter or serving plates, and spoon the dressing over the top. Sprinkle the toasted pepitas over that.

Serves 6–8.

# Chicken Tamale Bake with Jalapeno Smashed Potatoes

2 tablespoons olive oil

2 cups minced white onion

4 skinless and boneless chicken breasts, split into 8 pieces

3 cups water

1/2 cup fresh chopped parsley

2 tablespoons salt or to taste

1 tablespoon fresh cracked pepper

3 cups masa de harina

2 tablespoons ground cumin

2 tablespoons mild chili powder

2 cups minced prepared green chilies (mild)

6 large potatoes, peeled, quartered, and poached in salted water
  until tender, drained

8 jalapeno peppers, peeled, seeded, and split in half (Wear rubber
  gloves when handling hot peppers.)

6 large egg whites

1 teaspoon soy sauce

1 tablespoon sweet paprika

Heat oil in a large sauté pan over medium-high heat and stir in onion. Sauté onion until golden, and arrange chicken pieces in pan over onion. Cook chicken 2 minutes, turn chicken, and pour water, parsley, salt, and pepper over chicken. Cover pan, and reduce heat to medium. Simmer 50 minutes or until chicken is very tender. Remove chicken, reserve broth, cool chicken, and cut up into small pieces. Stir masa de harina into broth with cumin and chili powder until smooth. Press into even layer of oiled 11 x 14-inch baking dish. Sprinkle chicken and chopped green chilies over the top.

Mash the potatoes. Toast the jalapeno halves in a small, nonstick sauté pan over medium-high heat about 4 minutes, skin will be blistered. Mince. Mix jalapeno into potatoes along with egg whites, soy sauce, and paprika. Beat with electric hand mixer until fluffy and spread over chicken and green chilies.

Bake in preheated 325 degree oven until top is golden brown and slightly crisp, about 40 minutes. Serve hot.

Serves 8–10.

## Pinto Beans with Plantains and Cilantro

1 tablespoon safflower oil

1 cup minced onion

2 tablespoons fresh minced garlic

1/2 cup chopped seeded sweet yellow peppers

30 ounces, (2 cans) prepared pinto beans, drained

1 tablespoon mild chili powder or to taste

1 tablespoon ground cumin

1/2 cup fresh chopped cilantro

2 ripe plantains, peeled and slightly mashed

1 cup Monterey Jack cheese (or fat free mozzarella), shredded

In a large, heavy skillet over medium-high heat, heat oil and brown the onion, garlic, and yellow pepper. Reduce heat to medium and stir in beans. Cook 3 or 4 minutes. Stir in the remaining ingredients except cheese, and reduce heat to medium-low. Cook until very hot, top with cheese, and serve. You may also pour into a baking dish, top with cheese, cover, and refrigerate then bake until bubbly when ready to serve.

Serves 8–10.

## Pico de Gallo

1 cup fresh chopped mild green chili (Anaheim peppers are great)

1 cup chopped seeded firm tomato

1 cup chopped yellow onion

1 cup fresh chopped cilantro

juice from 2 limes

Mix together all ingredients.

Makes about 3 cups.

## Cinnamon Meringues with Fresh Strawberry Sauce

*For the meringues:*

6 large egg whites

1 teaspoon cream of tartar

1½ cups granulated sugar

1 tablespoon ground cinnamon

*Low Fat
Southwestern
for Geraldo
Rivera*

Beat egg whites on low speed with electric hand beaters, and add cream of tartar. Raise speed to medium-high and beat until they begin to get frothy. Very gradually add the sugar while beating and beat until stiff peaks are formed, then beat in cinnamon. Place meringue in pastry tube (in batches, if necessary) fitted with star or decorative tip. Pipe into desired shapes onto parchment paper lined baking sheets and place into 250 degree oven for 30 minutes. Reduce heat to 200 and bake until crisp, about 4 hours or overnight. They should be very crisp but not browned. Keep in warm oven or airtight container until ready to serve.

Makes about 18–24 meringues.

*For the strawberry sauce:*
2 pints strawberries, trimmed and rinsed
1 1/2 cups granulated sugar

Place strawberries in heavy saucepan over medium heat and stir in sugar. Heat until sugar dissolves, stir again, and simmer 10 minutes. Remove from heat to heat-proof bowl and cool to room temperature. Cover and refrigerate up to 3 days before serving.

Makes about 2 1/2 cups.

*To serve:*
Make pools of strawberry sauce on pretty plates, and arrange meringues on top. Garnish with fresh strawberries.

# Spicy Summer Supper

Perfect for outdoor dining, this menu will spice up any summer night's gathering. The crisp, delicious, and pepper zapped soft shell crabs are great with a salad for lunch and will leave your guests talking. If there are any left over, wrap them in foil and refrigerate. Heat them up the next day in the oven, and make them into a sandwich with mayonnaise and sour dough bread. Awesome!

—— *hints* ——

- Without a doubt, purchase live crabs and have them cleaned at the fish market. Frozen ones will do in a pinch, but there is nothing like fresh.

- Make the dipping sauce and Mango Chile Chutney along with the raspberry citrus sauce the day before. The crabs are best when prepared just before enjoying.

- Use fresh or refrigerated packaged pasta and have a pot of simmering water on a few minutes before your guests arrive.

# m • e • n • u

## Cajun Soft Shell Crabs with Quick Curry Dipping Sauce

## Mango Chile Chutney with Baby Greens

## Angel Hair Pasta with Fresh Tomatoes, Basil, and Garlic

## Raspberry Citrus Sundae

# Cajun Soft Shell Crabs

8 medium fresh soft shell crabs, cleaned (preferably by the person
   from whom they are purchased)

3 large eggs

1 cup corn starch

up to 1 cup milk

1 teaspoon sweet paprika

1 tablespoon chili powder

salt and fresh cracked pepper to taste

2 tablespoons minced garlic

safflower oil for frying

Rinse crabs and pat dry. Slightly beat the eggs. Mix the cornstarch with the milk by gradually adding just enough to make
a smooth paste. Stir egg into milk/cornstarch mixture. Add paprika,
chili powder, salt, and pepper.

Heat over medium-high heat enough oil in a large, deep, heavy
skillet to create a depth of 1/4 inch. Stir garlic into oil. Dip a crab
in egg mixture and gently place in the hot oil. Repeat with balance of crabs, frying 2 or 3 at a time. They are done when nicely
browned on both sides, about 2½ minutes per side. Keep warm on
paper towel until all are finished and serve as soon as possible.

Serves 4.

——— *hints* ———
*cont.*

- **You can bring the
  water to a boil and
  cook the pasta easily
  just before it is to
  be served.**

——— *words of* ———
*appreciation*

*A warm breeze and spicy
cuisine. A warm heart
and a spicy glance. The
balance of nature and
communication are art
forms in life. We are blessed
to be part of the harmony.*

# Quick Curry Dipping Sauce

1 cup mayonnaise

2 tablespoons sweet pickle relish

1 tablespoon catsup

curry powder to taste

Mix together, cover, and refrigerate until ready to serve.

Makes a generous cupful.

 # Mango Chile Chutney with Baby Greens

1 mango, firm but ripe

fresh chopped cilantro to taste

minced jalapeno pepper to taste

16 to 20 ounces baby salad greens

1/2 cup onion, minced

juice from 2 limes

salt and pepper to taste

Cut mango in wedges and separate from pit. Slice meat down to skin in a grid work and then cut along the skin to free mango chunks. Toss with balance of ingredients, cover, and refrigerate until ready to serve.

Serves 6–8.

# Angel Hair Pasta with Fresh Tomatoes, Basil, and Garlic

salted water for boiling pasta

2 tablespoons extra virgin olive oil

1 tablespoon (or more, to taste) fresh minced or thinly sliced garlic

1 pound dry or 2 pounds fresh angel hair pasta

4 to 6 firm ripe tomatoes, seeded and chopped

1 cup fresh minced basil leaves

1/4 cup white or red wine

salt and pepper to taste

freshly grated Parmesan cheese to taste

Bring salted water to low boil. Heat oil in large, heavy sauté pan over medium-high heat and stir in garlic to sauté until golden. Lower heat to medium. Bring water to full boil, and start cooking pasta. Add tomatoes and basil to pan with oil and garlic, stir in wine, and season with salt and pepper. Reduce to simmer. When pasta is al dente, drain and toss with tomato sauce. Serve with Parmesan.

Serves 6–8 as a side dish.

# Raspberry Citrus Sundae

| | |
|---|---|
| 2 pints raspberries | 1 cup sugar |
| zest from 1 lemon | ice cream of choice |
| zest from 1 lime | whipped topping of choice |
| juice from 1 lime | Pirouette cookies for garnish |

Rinse raspberries and combine in heavy saucepan over medium heat with the zests, lime juice, and sugar. Bring to simmer and allow to cook, stirring just a time or two, for 10 minutes. Cool in heat-proof bowl, cover, and refrigerate until ready to use.

Scoop ice cream into serving dishes, and ladle raspberry sauce over the top. Top with whipped topping, and garnish with cookie.

Makes about 2 cups of sauce, enough for 6–8 sundaes.

# Thai Hollywood Holiday Banquet with Downtown Julie Brown

*Julie Brown lives the Hollywood dream. And a dream is all she had just a few years ago. But now, a successful television personality and actress, her beauty is only a small part of what she has going for her. Her lifestyle is fast and her pace furious. She is taking the fantasy ride as far as it will go, shoot to shoot and city to city.*

And when she is home and ready to party, party she does. I was the one living a dream the night we cooked together. Her friends are beautiful. Her home is beautiful. Her view is beautiful. She is beautiful. Her world is beautiful. And for this evening, she showed me the happening side of Hollywood. I partied for and with the beautiful people!

*Thai Hollywood
Holiday Banquet
with Downtown
Julie Brown*

──── *hints* ────

- This is an ambitious menu. Be in the mood to cook and have a lot of time. Prepare all of your ingredients, and get as much done ahead of time as you can.

- You can purchase the sorbet if there is a gourmet ice cream parlor around.

- If you are pressed for time, purchase the spring rolls, and buy the cooked rice to make into the toasted rice. The spring rolls can be assembled ahead of time, covered, and refrigerated until you are ready to fry them and the won tons.

# m • e • n • u

Wasabi Teriyaki Nuts

Cello Noodle and Cabbage Spring Rolls

Peppered Peanut Dipping Sauce

Fermented Black Bean Tapenade with
Fried Won Tons

Peanut Sesame Tofu with Scallions

Curried Sesame Yams with Apricot Glaze

Toasted Rice with Sprouts, Saffron,
Red Pepper, and Mint

Coconut Sorbet

# Wasabi Teriyaki Nuts

1 tablespoon safflower oil

1 tablespoon fresh minced garlic

8 ounces raw shelled hazel nuts

8 ounces raw shelled Brazil nuts

1 tablespoon low sodium soy sauce

1/8 cup granulated turbinado sugar

cracked pepper and wasabi powder to taste

Heat oil in a large, heavy, nonstick sauté pan over medium-high heat and stir in garlic. When garlic begins to turn golden, reduce heat to medium and stir in nuts and toast, stirring occasionally, about 7 minutes. Drizzle soy sauce over nuts. Sprinkle sugar, pepper, and wasabi over nuts and stir to coat.

Makes about 3 cups of nuts.

# Cello Noodle and Cabbage Spring Rolls

6 cups boiling water

4 ounces bean threads (cello noodles)

2 cups finely shredded white or Savoy cabbage

1 cup fresh chopped cilantro leaves

1 tablespoon fresh minced garlic

1 tablespoon fresh minced ginger

2 tablespoons Hoisin sauce

1 tablespoon low sodium soy sauce

——— *hints* ———
*cont.*

- The dipping sauce and tapenade can be made a day in advance. If you are able, have someone come by and help serve and clean up. You may just want to relax with your guests and be waited on after this masterpiece. Besides, you won't want to miss a single accolade!

——— *words of* ———
*appreciation*

*Ciao, Baby!*

*Thai Hollywood
Holiday Banquet
with Downtown
Julie Brown*

1 tablespoon toasted sesame seeds

milled Szechwan peppercorn to taste

1 pound egg roll wrappers

safflower oil for deep frying

Boil the bean threads in the water for 60 seconds. Drain and rinse under cold water to cool. Drain and cut up noodles into short lengths (use the scissors or kitchen sheers). Toss with cabbage, cilantro, garlic, ginger, Hoisin, soy sauce, sesame seeds, and Szechwan pepper. Divide filling among wrappers and roll up to form tight egg rolls as usually directed on wrapper package.

Heat enough oil to have four or five inches in depth in a large, deep, heavy pot or deep fryer. When oil is hot, fry spring roll in batches until all are crisp and browned. Remove to paper towels to drain and hold briefly in warm oven until all are fried.

Makes 12 large spring rolls.

 ## Peppered Peanut Dipping Sauce

1 cup chunky peanut butter

1 cup seasoned rice vinegar (as for sushi)

1 tablespoon fresh minced garlic

1 tablespoon fresh minced ginger

1 dash soy sauce or to taste

Blend ingredients together well. Cover and refrigerate until ready to serve.

Makes about 2 cups.

## Fermented Black Bean Tapenade with Fried Won Tons

2 cups low sodium pitted black olives

1 tablespoon fresh minced garlic

1 teaspoon dried lemon grass

4 ounces fermented black bean sauce

1 teaspoon fresh lemon juice

Place all ingredients in bowl of food processor fitted with steel blade. Pulse until almost smooth. Serve with fried won tons or endive leaves.

Makes about 2 cups.

## Peanut Sesame Tofu with Scallions

20 ounces firm tofu, sliced into 1/2-inch thick slices

safflower oil for sautéing tofu slices

1 tablespoon peanut oil

3 tablespoons fresh minced garlic

3 tablespoons fresh minced ginger

1 cup salted dry roasted peanuts

1 jar Hoisin sauce (8 to 10 ounces)

1/4 cup vegetable stock

1 tablespoon soy sauce

1/2 cup toasted sesame seeds

1 cup chopped scallions

Pat the tofu slices dry and sauté in hot safflower oil 1-inch deep until golden brown on both sides, turning slices as needed. Remove to paper towel to drain. When cool enough to handle, cut into bite-sized rectangles. Heat peanut oil in wok or large, heavy sauté pan over high heat and stir in garlic, ginger, and peanuts. Sauté about 3 minutes. Reduce heat to medium and stir in Hoisin, stock, soy sauce, and finally tofu. Sprinkle with sesame seeds and scallions and stir in to mix. Serve immediately.

Serves 6–8.

## Curried Sesame Yams with Apricot Glaze

4 large or 6 medium yams

1 tablespoon safflower oil

2 tablespoons Nori Komi Furikake or 1 tablespoon each of white sesame seed, black sesame seed, and seaweed shake

1 tablespoon peanut oil

1 medium white onion, minced

2 tablespoons sweet curry blend of choice

1 cup vegetable stock

1 tablespoon soy sauce

1/2 cup apricot preserves

1 cup fresh chopped scallions

Peel yams and cut up as for thick French fries. Toss with safflower oil and Nori Komi Furikake and place in one layer on a non-stick jelly roll pan. Roast potatoes in preheated 325 degree oven until tender, about 45 minutes.

Heat peanut oil in wok or large, nonstick, heavy skillet, and sauté onions until golden. Stir in curry, and reduce heat to medium. Stir in stock, soy sauce, and preserves. Toss sauce with potatoes and scallions. Serve immediately.

Serves 6–8 as a side dish.

##  Toasted Rice with Sprouts, Saffron, Red Pepper, and Mint

2 cups jasmine rice

3 1/2 cups boiling water

1 cup vegetable stock

2 tablespoons low sodium soy sauce

1/4 teaspoon crumbled saffron threads

1 tablespoon dried lemon grass

2 tablespoons fresh minced garlic

12 ounces fresh bean sprouts

1 cup fresh diced red bell pepper

1 cup fresh mint leaves

1 cup fresh minced scallions

Place rice in boiling water, and reduce heat to simmer. Cover tightly and simmer 20 minutes. Turn off heat and allow to stand five minutes. Fluff rice with fork. Spray a nonstick jelly roll pan with cooking spray, and spread rice in a semi-even layer

*Thai Hollywood
Holiday Banquet
with Downtown
Julie Brown*

without pressing on rice. Place in preheated 325 degree oven for 45 to 60 minutes until rice begins to crisp around edges. In a wok or large pot over high heat, heat stock, soy sauce, saffron, lemon grass, and garlic. Toss in rice and stir fry with remaining ingredients. Serve hot.

Serves 6–8.

 ## Coconut Sorbet

40 ounces coconut milk
8 ounces thread coconut
1 cup sugar

Combine ingredients in heavy saucepan over medium heat and simmer until coconut is soft and tender, about 35 minutes. Cool to room temperature, cover, and chill in refrigerator. Place mix in ice cream or sorbet maker and freeze as directed.

Makes about 6 cups of sorbet.

# Slim South of the Border Fiesta

*This menu was originally designed for two, my wife and me. We had just finished running six miles on a tropical Treasure Coast (Southeast Florida Coast) summer day. Both ravenous, neither of us wanted to undo our energetic efforts in satisfying our appetites. I jumped in the car after lighting the gas grill and was back in twenty minutes with the necessities for the following "created on the way to the store" menu including the now hot grill. And, by the look in Laurie's eyes, I knew I had to set a record for turning raw chicken breasts into fajitas. The fat free tortillas were warming just as I caught her reaching for the ice cream, and she thanked me for it later. And, of course, those "thank yous" are the real reason I cook!*

*chef harry & friends*

*Slim South of the Border Fiesta*

## —— hints ——

- The Black Bean and Corn Salad and Quick White Salsa can be made a day in advance.

- You can also make the fajitas without the chicken or use leftover meat or fish.

- In a hurry, you can use the quick brown rice. Either way, the rice can be made earlier in the day and reheated before serving.

# m • e • n • u

Quick White Salsa

Chicken Fajitas

Brown Rice with Scallions

Black Bean and Corn Salad

Papaya Marshmallow Parfait

 Quick White Salsa

1 cup fat free sour cream

1/2 cup jalapeno stuffed olives, drained and chopped

1/2 cup chopped red onion

1 tablespoon chili powder or to taste

Mix ingredients together. Keep refrigerated until ready to serve.

Makes about 1½ cups.

 Chicken Fajitas

4 skinless, boneless chicken breasts, trimmed and split
   into 8 halves

1 teaspoon fresh ground cumin

1 teaspoon fresh minced garlic

1 teaspoon extra virgin olive oil

2 bell peppers, trimmed and sliced thinly

1 teaspoon mild chili powder

2 sweet onions, sliced

juice from 4 limes

2 teaspoons light soy sauce

8 flour tortillas (the fat free ones are fine)

Rinse chicken in cold water and place in zipper lock bag with lime juice, 1 teaspoon of the soy sauce, cumin, chili powder, garlic, and olive oil. Seal bag and shake to coat and marinate. Refrigerate up to 24 hours if desired. Grill over medium-hot coals

—— words of ——
a p p r e c i a t i o n

*As we enjoy the
pleasures of life together, we
give thanks for each other
and the life we have built
together from the blessings
bestowed upon us.*

until just done, about 4 to 5 minutes per side. Remove to platter and hold in warm oven.

Spray large, heavy, nonstick sauté pan with cooking spray and heat over high heat until hot. Stir in peppers and onions and drizzle with 1/2 of the remaining teaspoon of soy sauce. Stir contents of pan over high heat for 2 minutes. Remove from heat and cover to steam vegetables. Meanwhile, slice chicken. Move peppers and onions to one side of pan, and place sliced chicken on the other. Heat over high heat until steaming, and drizzle last of soy sauce over pan. Wrap tortillas in a towel and warm on high in the microwave for 45 seconds. Serve filling with warm tortillas.

Serves 6–8.

## Brown Rice with Scallions

2 tablespoons canola oil
1 cup chopped white onion
1 teaspoon fresh minced garlic
1 tablespoon salt
2 cups brown rice
water per directions for rice (about 3½ cups), some brands vary a bit
1 cup chopped fresh scallions—white and greens

Heat oil in heavy saucepan, and brown onion and garlic. Stir in salt and rice and sauté 2 minutes. Stir in water, cover and simmer over low until water is absorbed and rice is tender, about 30 to 40 minutes. Stir in scallions and serve.

Serves 6–8.

# Black Bean and Corn Salad

3 cups canned black beans, drained and rinsed

2 cups yellow corn kernels, drained or thawed and rinsed

1 tablespoon fresh minced garlic

1 cup chopped white onion

1 cup chopped seeded sweet yellow or green chile or bell pepper

1/4 cup fresh chopped cilantro

2 tablespoons ground cumin

juice from 3 limes

salt and pepper to taste

Toss ingredients together, cover, and refrigerate up to 24 hours before serving.

Serves 6–8.

 # Papaya Marshmallow Parfait

2 fresh papayas, seeded

1 quart fat free vanilla ice cream, softened

1 jar marshmallow fluff

fresh strawberries for garnish

Mash the papaya into the ice cream, and alternate ice cream with marshmallow fluff in parfait glasses. Serve with strawberries as a garnish.

Makes 6–8 parfaits.

# Serious Supper For Funny Phyllis Diller

*Phyllis Diller is many things. Actress, Comedienne, mother, artist, fund-raiser, friend, and hostess. When I arrived at her home for some fun with the legendary comic, I discovered just what kind of hostess she is. Her sprawling Brentwood estate was built by Senator Phipps and was created for parties. Spacious, elegantly appointed rooms and a dining room table that seated twenty comfortably (there were probably more leaves for the table in the closet!). Many of the rooms had their French doors flung open to a center courtyard with a carved stone fountain like something from a piazza in Italy.*

Entering her kitchen, there was no doubt that Phyllis is also an accomplished cook. "I just stay away from things that go in the oven. I'm fine on top of the stove, but when I put things in that darn oven, they always come out burned!" I knew she was pulling my leg, and her daughter, Stephanie, there to manage some of the hectic affairs of the household, confirmed that growing up she always enjoyed her mother's creations.

My interview with Phyllis was one of the first of my career, and we have since become friends. She is one of Hollywood's greats, with a heart to match her success. I have learned a lot from her in a very short time. She always has a smile, a laugh, and a moment for everyone.

*Serious Supper
for Funny
Phyllis Diller*

# m • e • n • u

Drunken Seafood Medley

Curried Cucumber and Caper Chutney in
Belgian Endive Leaves

Smoked Salmon Bruschetta

Italian Greens, Purple Grapes, and Blue
Goat Cheese with Toasted Pecan Vinaigrette

Apricot Shallot Glazed Pork

Coconut Currant Chutney

Leek Pudding

Pecan Praline Tiramisu

--- *hints* ---

- This ambitious menu can be tapered down and still be impressive. Omit the Smoked Salmon Bruschetta, and buy a dessert if you like.
- The vinaigrette, glaze for the pork, chutney, and tiramisu can be made the day before.
- The Leek Pudding can be assembled the day before and baked prior to serving.
- The pudding and salad together make a wonderful lunch on a fall day.

## Drunken Seafood Medley

1 cup cocktail shrimp

1 cup cooked lobster meat, cut into chunks

1 cup mild pepperoncini, stems removed and drained

1 cup garlic stuffed olives, drained

1 cup trimmed, fresh shredded and rinsed fennel

1/8 cup fresh chopped dill

1 cup good quality vodka

salt and pepper to taste

Toss all ingredients, cover, and chill up to 24 hours before serving.

Serves 6–8.

## Curried Cucumber and Caper Chutney in Belgian Endive Leaves

1 cup chopped, peeled, and seeded English cucumber

1/2 cup giant capers, drained

1 teaspoon dried oregano

1 teaspoon ground cumin

1 teaspoon mild curry powder or curry powder blend

3/4 cup creme fraiche or sour cream

20-24 Belgian endive leaves, trimmed, rinsed, and patted dry

Toss ingredients except for creme fraiche, and endive. Carefully stir creme fraiche into cucumber mixture. When ready to serve, divide among endive leaves.

Serves 8–12.

———*words of*———
*appreciation*

*We all walk down the same paths as legends and as those less fortunate. Those of us who are truly thankful for life's blessings try to bring a smile to all we meet.*

*chef harry & friends*

*Serious Supper
for Funny
Phyllis Diller*

## Smoked Salmon Bruschetta

4 medium tomatoes, seeded and chopped

1 tablespoon fresh minced garlic

3/4 cup fresh chopped basil leaves

1 tablespoon extra virgin olive oil

juice from 1 lemon

salt and pepper to taste

16 Garlic Crostini (page 33)

16 thin slices smoked salmon

Toss together the tomato, garlic, basil, oil, lemon juice, and salt and pepper. Divide among crostini, and top each with a slice of salmon, loosely rolled up attractively.

Serves 8.

## Italian Greens, Purple Grapes, and Blue Goat Cheese with Toasted Pecan Vinaigrette

2 tablespoons extra virgin olive oil

1 tablespoon fresh minced garlic

1 cup shelled pecan halves

2 tablespoons sugar

1 cup red wine vinegar

1 cup fresh shredded basil leaves

salt and pepper to taste

1 cup safflower oil

12–18 ounces mixed baby greens, rinsed and dried

1 cup seedless purple grapes, sliced in half lengthwise

2/3 cup fresh crumbled goat cheese

2/3 cup crumbled blue cheese

chef harry & friends

*Serious Supper*
*for Funny*
*Phyllis Diller*

Heat olive oil in saucepan over medium-high heat and stir in garlic. Sauté for 2 minutes and stir in pecans. Sauté 2 minutes more. Remove from heat, cool for 5 minutes, and stir in sugar, vinegar, basil, salt, and pepper. Stir in safflower oil, toss with greens, grapes, and cheeses.

Serves 8.

## Apricot Shallot Glazed Pork

*For the glaze:*
1 tablespoon extra virgin olive oil
1/2 cup fresh chopped shallot
1/4 cup soy sauce
20 to 24 ounces apricot preserves

In a heavy saucepan over medium-high heat, heat oil and stir in shallots. Sauté until shallots begin to brown. Reduce heat to low and stir in soy sauce and preserves. Bring to a simmer. Use or remove to glass bowl, cover, and refrigerate up to 3 days until ready to use.

Makes 2$^1/_2$ cups.

*To glaze chops:*
8 butterflied pork tenderloin filets
1 tablespoon extra virgin olive oil
2 tablespoons fresh minced garlic
1 tablespoon soy sauce
1 cup orange juice

Toss all ingredients together and allow to marinate up to 24 hours. Heat coals in grill until very hot, and heat grill surface as well. Sear pork chops over hot coals for 2 minutes on each side, dipping in warm glaze as removed from grill. Arrange in roasting pan in a single layer, pour remaining glaze over chops, and roast in preheated 325 degree oven until done, about 20 minutes for well-done.

 ## Coconut Currant Chutney

1 tablespoon extra virgin olive oil

1/2 cup minced onion

1 tablespoon fresh minced garlic

1 cup currants

1 cup shredded coconut, unsweetened

1/2 cup granulated sugar

1/2 cup drinking sherry

1/2 to 1 cup water

Heat oil in heavy saucepan over medium-high heat and stir in onion and sauté until onions begin to brown around the edges. Stir in garlic and sauté one minute more. Reduce heat to low and stir in currants, coconut, and sugar. Slowly stir in sherry, and raise heat to medium. Slowly add water and bring to simmer. Cook until currants and coconut are tender, adding more water if necessary, about 10 minutes.

Makes 2$\frac{1}{2}$ cups.

 ## Leek Pudding

1 cup unsalted butter

5 to 6 cups leeks, cleaned and sliced into small pieces

2 tablespoons fresh minced garlic

salt and pepper to taste

1 cup dry sherry

4 cups chicken or vegetable stock

1 day old baguette, sliced into 2-inch thick pieces

2 cups shredded fontina or mozzarella cheese

1 cup shredded Parmesan cheese

2 tablespoons melted butter

Serious Supper
for Funny
Phyllis Diller

Heat 1 cup butter in heavy soup pot over medium-high heat and stir in leeks and garlic. Season with salt and pepper and sauté until leeks are tender, about 5 minutes. Reduce heat to medium and pour in sherry. Reduce heat to low, place a piece of foil directly on onions to "sweat" them for about an hour. Stir in stock and remove from heat.

Arrange bread in a single layer in a buttered baking dish to accommodate. Ladle leeks over bread slices and top with fontina and Parmesan. Drizzle melted butter over casserole and bake in preheated 350 oven until cheese is brown and bubbly.

Serves 8–12.

# Pecan Praline Tiramisu

2 pounds mascarpone cheese

1 pound pecan pralines, pulverized in a food processor

1½ cups Kahlua

1/8 cup cooled double strength espresso

1 cup powdered sugar

1 cup heavy whipping cream

2 cups lady finger crumbs

1 cup pecans, pulverized

1 tablespoon cinnamon

chocolate dipped strawberries for garnish (optional)

Whip the mascarpone with the praline crumbs, 1 cup Kahlua, and espresso. Slowly add the sugar and beat in whipping cream until light and fluffy, 2 or 3 minutes.

Toss to combine the lady finger crumbs, pecans, and cinnamon. Drizzle the 1/2 cup Kahlua over that and toss to mix. Divide this mixture among 12 champagne flutes or wine glasses. Place mascarpone mixture in a pastry bag fitted with a star or decorative tip. Pipe among glasses on top of crumbs and top with strawberry, if desired. Chill until ready to serve. Can be made 24 hours in advance.

Makes 12.

# Picnic by the Pool

*This is a wonderful family menu. Living on or near the beach for a good part of our marriage, Laurie and I love to entertain outside and make a day of it with friends who have kids around our daughter Alexa's age. The baked salami is one of the easiest things to make and serve, and everyone goes nuts for it. A friend of ours from Des Moines, Iowa introduced me to her version, which she credited to Julia Child. Whoever thought of it, I get more compliments on this simple snack than things I spend hours creating!*

**chef harry & friends**

*Picnic by
the Pool*

—— *hints* ——

- The crudité dip, the
  Dijon Dipping Sauce,
  and the meltaways
  can be made a day
  in advance.

- Pick up a rosemary,
  olive, or other interesting
  baguette for a more
  exciting sub.

# m•e•n•u

Quick Crudité

Dijon Dipping Sauce

Garlic Baked Salami

Grilled Chicken and Guacamole Subs

Chocolate Peanut Butter Meltaways

 ## Quick Crudité

2 cups sour cream (low fat or fat free is fine)

1/2 cup chopped scallions

2 tablespoons fresh minced garlic

1 cup fresh chopped basil

1 teaspoon dried oregano

salt and pepper to taste

assorted vegetables for dipping (the prepared ones in bags
   work great)

Mix together the sour cream with everything but the vegetables for dipping. Hollow out a cabbage or kale to serve dip in, if desired, and attractively arrange vegetables around dip.

Makes about 3 cups dip, enough for veggies for 12. (Dip also goes great in baked potatoes!)

 ## Dijon Dipping Sauce

1 cup mayonnaise

2 tablespoons Dijon mustard

1 tablespoon catsup

Mix together well. Cover and refrigerate until ready to serve.

Makes a little over a cup.

—— *w o r d s   o f* ——
*a p p r e c i a t i o n*

*Looking into our children's eyes, we can see the future and the past. Our children are our lives, and through their happiness comes our own. May they always feel and be protected by the support of our love.*

## Garlic Baked Salami

1 large all beef salami
6 garlic cloves

Make a 1-inch deep slit down the length of the salami. Slice the garlic cloves in two, and insert the garlic halves in the slit. Bake the salami on a tray in a preheated 325 degree oven for 2 to 3 hours, until crisp on the outside and still juicy on the inside. Slice when cool enough to handle. Serve with Dijon Dipping Sauce.

## Grilled Chicken and Guacamole Subs

*For the chicken:*

2 skinless, boneless chicken breasts, split into 2 pieces each
1 tablespoon soy sauce
1 tablespoon extra virgin olive oil
1 tablespoon fresh minced garlic

Place ingredients in zipper lock bag and toss to marinate. Refrigerate up to 24 hours. Grill chicken over medium-hot coals until juices run clear, about 4 minutes per side. Cool and refrigerate until slicing to assemble sub.

*For the guacamole:*

3 ripe avocados
1/4 cup minced sweet onion
1/4 cup minced red bell pepper

1/4 cup fresh chopped cilantro leaves

1 seeded and chopped tomato

1 teaspoon ground cumin

1 teaspoon ground sweet chili powder

Mash the avocado with all ingredients to combine. If not to be eaten right away, place seeds from avocado in guacamole and cover with plastic wrap directly touching guacamole and refrigerate.

To assemble subs:

1 large baguette

2 cups mixed greens, rinsed

Slice a lengthwise "top" off of the baguette and set aside. Remove a good deal of the bread from the crust creating a well. Spread the guacamole in the well. (Use any extra with chips for dip.) Slice chicken and arrange on top of guacamole. Top with lettuce, and replace bread "top." Slice, serve.

Serves 6–8.

# Chocolate Peanut Butter Meltaways

1 stick butter

1 cup graham cracker crumbs

12 ounces chocolate chips

1 cup chopped cocktail peanuts (use the food processor for chopping)

12 ounces peanut butter chips

7 ounces sweetened flaked coconut

1 can sweetened condensed milk

Melt butter in 9 x 12-inch baking dish. Sprinkle crumbs over butter, the chocolate chips over crumbs, peanuts over chocolate, peanut butter chips over peanuts, coconut over peanut butter chips, and pour milk in an even layer on top. Bake in pre-heated 350 degree oven until coconut toasts, about 40 minutes. Cool and cut into squares.

Makes 24 pieces.

# South African Holiday Supper with James Earl Jones

*James Earl Jones and his wife, Ce Ce, were my first celebrity "at home" interview. This was also my first time making ostrich. It was my first time in their kitchen. It was my first article for the magazine for which I was there to write. Between cooking for a legend, photographers flashing in my face, NBC's Extra coming by, I would say that the entire experience was full of firsts!*

The Joneses were not there when I arrived, which was great, as it gave me some time to get settled, organized, set the table, and arrange the flowers. I was just learning how to throw an elaborate party out of a suitcase at the time. James' billowing voice arrived before they did. It was like an announcement of royalty on the approach. As they joined me in their kitchen, it was quite apparent that they were as anxious to eat as I was to feed them. They made me feel right at home, and we got down to cooking.

Maybe it was the time of year, maybe it was their mood, maybe it was just the Food Gods watching over me, but everything just came out great. There I was, glazing ostrich tenderloin in the kitchen with James Earl Jones and his wife, having the time of my life.

I think that it was on that day, after seeing how charming and down to earth a real celebrity and his wife could be, that I decided how much fun I could have as a celebrity chef. I am still having that kind of fun today!

South African
Holiday Supper with
James Earl Jones

— hints —

- This special occasion menu requires some extra planning if it is to be reproduced as is. Finding ostrich tenderloin and Wild Boar Blueberry Sausage can be perplexing, but you may substitute beef for the ostrich and grilled Italian sausage instead of the boar sausage.

- The Curried Pickled Fish, beet salad, chutney, and coconut custard can be made the day ahead.

- You may also make the corn bread in advance and sauté just before serving.

# m•e•n•u

Curried Pickled Fish

Sweet Potato Coconut Soup with Wild Boar
Blueberry Sausage

Salad of Pickled Chopped Beet, Green
Beans, and Onion

Glazed Tenderloin of Ostrich

Apricot, Date, and Vidalia Chutney

Dutch Style Cabbage with
Granny Smith Apples

Sautéed Corn Pepper Bread

Brandied Coconut Custard with Currants

# Curried Pickled Fish

1 cup canola or safflower oil

1 pound haddock or sole fillets

1 large onion, peeled and thinly sliced

1 jalapeno pepper, trimmed, seeded, and minced (Wear rubber
gloves when handling hot peppers.)

1 tablespoon fresh chopped garlic

2 tablespoons fresh minced ginger

1 tablespoon sweet curry powder blend

1 teaspoon ground coriander

1/2 cup white vinegar

1/2 cup light brown or turbinado sugar

salt and pepper to taste

In a large, heavy, nonstick sauté pan, heat the oil over medium-high heat. Rinse and drain the fish and pat dry. Sauté fish in oil, turning once, until just done, about 2 minutes per side (fish will flake and be white throughout). Remove fish to paper towel to drain and cool.

Pour off oil from pan, leaving a glaze with any fish remains. Over medium-high heat, sauté onion for 5 minutes and stir in jalapeno pepper, garlic, ginger, and curry. Sauté 2 minutes more.

Reduce heat to low and stir in coriander, vinegar, and sugar. Stir until sugar is dissolved. Remove from heat and season with salt and pepper.

In a glass or ceramic bowl or jar, place 1/4 of the onion mixture in a layer on the bottom. Layer 1/2 of the fish over that. Layer 2/4 of the onion mixture over the fish, the remaining fish on that, and

——— *words of* ———
*appreciation*

*To comprehend the vastness of
creation is to comprehend life.
As we seek to broaden our
knowledge, we encounter that
which makes us grow.
Sharing that knowledge
makes the world a garden.*

the remaining onion on top of the second layer of fish. Cover and refrigerate 2 to 5 days.

Serves 6–8 as a first course.

## Sweet Potato Coconut Soup with Wild Boar Blueberry Sausage

5 medium yams, peeled, quartered, and poached until soft

1 cup unsweetened coconut milk

1 cup heavy cream

1/3 cup sugar

1 teaspoon each or to taste: ground cinnamon, clove, and nutmeg

1 pound boar sausage, grilled until well-done, cooled, and sliced
   (any good link sausage may be substituted)

In a food processor fitted with a steel blade, process yams with coconut milk until smooth.

Place in heavy, large saucepan over medium-low heat and stir in cream gradually. When hot but not boiling, stir in sugar and spices. Do not boil soup! Ladle hot soup into bowls and dot with slices of warmed sausage.

Serves 8.

# Salad of Pickled Chopped Beet, Green Beans, and Onion

2 cups red wine vinegar

2 cups water

1/2 cup granulated sugar

2 teaspoons dried oregano

2 tablespoons fresh minced garlic

2 tablespoons salt or to taste

fresh cracked pepper to taste

4 medium beets, peeled, quartered, and boiled in salted water
   until tender but not soft, drained and cooled

1 pound string beans, trimmed and boiled in salted water one
   minute, drained and cooled

1 medium white onion, sliced into strips

Mix together vinegar, water, sugar, oregano, garlic, salt, and pepper. Divide among 2 glass or ceramic containers, or pickling jars. Slice beets into shapes and place in one container with vinegar mixture adding water to cover beets, if necessary.

Slice string beans into small pieces and mix with onion in other container with vinegar. Cover and refrigerate both containers up to 4 days.

*To serve:*

Arrange beets around a mound of the chopped beans with onions. You may serve on mixed greens as well.

Serves 8.

# Glazed Tenderloin of Ostrich

4 pounds ostrich tenderloin, rinsed and patted dry

1/4 cup light soy sauce

1 tablespoon fresh minced garlic

1 tablespoon fresh minced ginger

2 tablespoons fresh cracked pepper

1 tablespoon canola oil

4 tablespoons garlic infused olive oil

6 cups chicken stock reduced (simmered) to 1 cup demi glace

Marinate ostrich in soy sauce mixed with garlic, ginger, pepper, and canola oil for up to 2 hours. On a very hot grill with cover, sear ostrich for 2 minutes on each side with lid down. Ostrich will be almost cooked at this point. Remove and cool. Wrap in plastic wrap and refrigerate until cold. Slice into 1/4-inch thick medallions. Heat 2 tablespoons of garlic oil in heavy, non-stick sauté pan over medium-high heat until hot. Arrange 1/2 of the medallions in the pan, and as soon as all are arranged, turn the medallions starting with the first one put in the pan. When all are turned, pour 1/2 cup of the demi glace over medallions and remove them to a warm platter. Repeat with other half of medallions and serve.

Serves 8.

## Apricot, Date, and Vidalia Chutney

2 tablespoons extra virgin olive oil

1 cup minced vidalia or other sweet onion

1 cup pitted and chopped dates

1 cup apricot preserves

Heat oil in a heavy, nonstick saucepan over medium-high heat. Stir in onion and sauté until onion begins to toast, about 6 minutes. Stir in dates, and reduce heat to medium-low. Stir in preserves, and bring contents to a simmer. Place in glass or ceramic bowl and cover until ready to serve. May be stored in refrigerator up to 5 days.

Makes about 2 cups.

## Dutch Style Cabbage with Granny Smith Apples

2 tablespoons extra virgin olive oil

1 medium white onion, chopped

1 medium red or white cabbage or 1 lb. bag of fresh preshredded
   prepared cabbage, rinsed

3 granny smith or other tart apples, peeled, cored, and sliced

1/2 cup red wine vinegar

1/2 cup light brown sugar

1 dash cinnamon (optional)

salt and pepper to taste

In a large, heavy pot with lid, heat the oil over medium-high heat and stir in onion. Sauté for 5 minutes, stirring frequently. Stir in cabbage and apples, cover, and reduce heat to medium-low. Cook for 20 minutes, stirring occasionally.

Remove cover from pan and stir in vinegar, sugar, and cinnamon. Season with salt and pepper and cover. Keep on low heat until ready to serve.

Serves 8.

 ## Sautéed Corn Pepper Bread

1/2 cup butter

1 medium yellow onion, chopped

1 green bell pepper, seeded and chopped

1 teaspoon salt

1 teaspoon fresh cracked pepper

1 cup corn kernels, frozen and thawed, canned, or fresh, rinsed
 and drained

6 cups water

1 cup corn meal

1 cup polenta

6 eggs, slightly beaten

garlic infused oil for oiling pan and sautéing bread

Heat butter in a large, deep pan over medium-high heat until foam subsides. Stir in onion, green pepper, salt, and pepper. Sauté until onion and green pepper are tender, about 6 minutes. Stir in corn and sauté 1 minute more.

Add water to pan and bring to boil. Reduce heat to medium-low and stir in corn meal and then polenta. When water is absorbed, remove pan from heat, and allow batter to rest 4 minutes. Quickly stir in eggs to combine well and scrape into large oiled loaf pan.

Bake in preheated 350 degree oven until bread puffs up and browns on top, about 40 to 50 minutes. Remove from oven and cool.

*To serve:*

Remove bread from pan and slice into 1-inch thick slices. Heat 1 tablespoon of garlic infused oil in a heavy, nonstick sauté pan over medium-high heat, and arrange bread slices in pan. Toast on both sides and serve warm.

Makes about 10 large pieces.

# Brandied Coconut Custard with Currants

1 14-ounce can sweetened condensed milk

8 ounces cream cheese, softened

1 cup heavy cream

6 egg yolks

1/8 cup brandy

1 teaspoon vanilla extract

1 cup shredded unsweetened coconut

1 cup currants

*South African
Holiday Supper with
James Earl Jones*

Place condensed milk, cream cheese, cream, egg yolks, brandy, and vanilla in a blender. Blend until smooth. Pour into 4 cup ovenproof baking dish. Place dish in larger ovenproof dish and surround with hot water up to 2 inches from top of smaller pan, if possible. Sprinkle coconut and currants on top of custard (they will sink to an even layer, which ends up as the top). Bake in pre-heated 325 degree oven about 1 hour or until center of custard seems firm and top begins to brown. Cover and cool before serving. Unmold onto serving platter. May be made 24 hours in advance.

Serves 8.

# Thanksgiving Leftover Makeover

*This menu came about for the Today show on NBC. They asked me to do a segment on making dishes out of Thanksgiving leftovers. I decided it should be a selection of recipes that would be on the holiday 'lite' side (less the ten million calories). After all, this is the day after the words "I am never eating again" ring out throughout America!*

## chef harry & friends

*Thanksgiving*
*Leftover*
*Makeover*

### — *hints* —

- If you use artichokes in your Thanksgiving feast, set enough aside to make the dip the next day.

- Have this meal planned when you do your shopping for Thanksgiving so you have all the requirements—no running to the market that morning!

# m • e • n • u

### Baked Artichoke Parmesan Dip

### Black Bean Turkey Burritos

### Cranberry Jalapeno Salsa

### Corn Dressing Fritters

### Raspberry Mousse Parfaits

## Baked Artichoke Parmesan Dip

2 small jars marinated artichoke hearts, drained and chopped

1 cup mayonnaise

1 cup shredded Parmesan

1 tablespoon fresh minced garlic

1 teaspoon Worcestershire sauce

1/2 cup bread crumbs

Stir together the artichokes, mayonnaise, Parmesan, garlic, and Worcestershire. Pour into an accommodating baking dish. Sprinkle crumbs on top. Bake in preheated 350 degree oven until brown and bubbly, about 30 minutes. Serve with crackers and flatbreads or tortilla chips.

Makes almost 3 cups.

 ## Black Bean Turkey Burritos

2 tablespoons olive or safflower oil

1 medium onion, chopped

1 tablespoon fresh minced garlic

1 15-ounce can prepared black beans, drained

1 16-ounce can fat free seasoned refried beans

1 tablespoon cumin powder

1 tablespoon mild chili powder

1 to 2 cups cooked turkey, cut into small pieces

1 cup shredded cheddar cheese (optional)

8 large flour tortillas, room temperature for pliability

—— *words of* ——
*appreciation*

*We have gathered together to appreciate the blessings of life. Each day's rising sun brings us more blessings. Each day we have more for which to be thankful.*

In a large, heavy, nonstick pan, heat 1 tablespoon oil over medium-high heat and stir in onion and garlic. Sauté 5 to 7 minutes or until golden brown. Reduce heat to medium and stir in beans, cumin, and chili powder, stirring until well mixed and hot. Turn off heat and stir in turkey and cheese just to mix.

Place a rectangle of the bean mixture in the center of a tortilla, and fold the bottom of the tortilla over the filling. Fold both ends toward the center and top over that to form the burrito. Repeat to form 8 burritos.

Heat the remaining tablespoon of oil in a large skillet or griddle. Brown both sides of the burritos, and heat the filling. Serve hot.

Makes 8 large burritos.

 ## Cranberry Jalapeno Salsa

1 teaspoon safflower oil

1 cup scallions, rinsed, trimmed, and chopped

2 jalapeno peppers, rinsed, trimmed, seeded, and chopped (Wear rubber gloves when handling hot peppers.)

2 cups cranberry sauce or relish

Heat safflower oil in heavy saucepan over medium-high heat. Stir in scallions and jalapeno and toast for a minute or two. Stir in cranberry relish and cook 5 minutes over medium heat. Remove to glass or ceramic bowl, cool, cover, and refrigerate until ready to serve.

Makes about 2$\frac{1}{2}$ cups.

## Corn Dressing Fritters

2 cups leftover dressing or stuffing

1½ cups corn kernels, frozen, canned, or fresh, rinsed and drained

3 large eggs or 6 egg whites

salt and pepper to taste

butter or vegetable oil for frying

Mix together the dressing, corn, eggs, salt, and pepper. You should be able to form small patties; add more egg if necessary. Heat butter or oil in a large, heavy, nonstick skillet over medium-high heat until hot. Form small patties of the mixture, and fry them in the oil until browned on both sides. Hold the finished patties in warm oven on foil or baking tray until ready to serve. They go great with barbecue sauce.

Makes about 12 patties serving 6–8.

 ## Raspberry Mousse Parfaits

1 small container fat free whipped topping

1 cup raspberry all fruit preserves

2 pints fresh raspberries, gently rinsed

Mix the topping with the preserves and layer with fresh raspberries in parfait glasses or champagne flutes. Garnish with more fresh raspberries, if desired.

Makes 6–8 parfaits.

# A Circus of a Meal with Ringling Brothers and Barnum & Bailey

Rare beef tenderloin on a spear for a tiger and fresh greens wrapped in large pitas for elephants; cooking for the stars of the circus brought a whole new meaning to the term celebrity chef! Although I found the tiger quite intimidating (why take a little meat on a stick when you can eat the man giving it to you?), the elephants were about the daintiest eaters I have ever fed. They were so gentle, and I found myself wanting to spend time getting to know them. Graham Thomas Chiperfield, eighth generation of Chiperfields in the circus, made it clear that they were not pets. It was his expert handling that made them so charming. That is why I fed Graham, too!

*chef harry & friends*

*A Circus of a Meal
with Ringling Brothers
and Barnum & Bailey*

—— *hints* ——

- The Caesar dressing
  can be made a day
  or two in advance
  and then tossed
  with the greens just
  before serving.

- The beef for the club
  can be grilled a day in
  advance. Always cool
  meat before slicing—
  that way it retains
  the juices.

- You may make the tarts
  with a graham cracker
  crust to save time.

# m • e • n • u

Caesar Salad Sandwich

Beef Tenderloin Club

Fresh Fruit Tarts

#  Caesar Salad Sandwich

4 cloves garlic

6 ounces anchovy filet

1 teaspoon Worcestershire sauce

1 teaspoon fresh cracked pepper

juice from 3 lemons

1 cup grated Parmesan cheese

1 cup extra virgin olive oil

16 ounces assorted fresh salad greens of choice, rinsed and dried

3 10 x 20-inch soft breads (lavosh)

Place garlic, anchovies, Worcestershire, pepper, lemon juice, and cheese in food processor fitted with steel blade. Pulse until well-combined. Process contents while gradually adding oil in a stream. Dressing should emulsify to the texture of mayonnaise after oil has been added.

Spread one side of each flat bread with the dressing. Divide greens on top, and roll sandwiches up tightly like jelly rolls. Wrap in plastic wrap and refrigerate up to 4 hours before serving. To serve, slice attractively on diagonal for pieces about 1 inch wide.

Makes about 36–42 finger sandwiches.

A Circus of a Meal
with Ringling Brothers
and Barnum & Bailey

——— w o r d s   o f ———
a p p r e c i a t i o n

*All creatures great and small share the earth and depend on each other to coexist. The respect for whom and where we coexist creates the harmony in life.*

*A Circus of a Meal*
*with Ringling Brothers*
*and Barnum & Bailey*

 Beef Tenderloin Club

3 hard boiled eggs, peeled

1/2 cup mayonnaise

1 tablespoon yellow mustard

12 ounces thinly sliced, rare, cold grilled beef tenderloin

2 thin slices purple onion

2 ounces fresh arugula

a crusty mini baguette or small sourdough loaf

Grate the eggs finely and combine with mayonnaise and mustard. Arrange with beef, onion, and arugula on bread.

Makes one huge sandwich.

 Fresh Fruit Tarts

1 10 to 12-inch baked tart shell or 8 individual shells

2 cups vanilla custard or pudding

3 cups assorted berries and sliced kiwi

1 cup apricot preserves

Spread the custard in an even layer in the bottom of the pastry shell. Arrange fruit attractively on top of custard. Heat preserves until they begin to simmer, and with a pastry brush, paint the fruit and drizzle the preserves over the tart to glaze entirely. Chill until ready to serve.

Serves 8–10.

# A Sunday Evening Supper on the Veranda

*In life, it is very lucky to meet a couple where all four of you hit it off. One such couple are dear friends of ours from Tulsa, Oklahoma. Susan and Jack are both very creative. She is a well-known international interior designer, and he is a world famous architect. They have helped us on many of our homes. They just have the knack for making things look perfect. Their style is one that sets trends.*

One night, they had us over to dinner, and Susan, being from Louisiana, announced in her merciless breathless femininity (Susan can say common words in a way that make men melt) that we would be "taking supper on the veranda." Well, I had lived in Tulsa many years and been to their house many times and "I ain't never seen no veranda." Come to find out that their veranda was what I called their back porch. What made it a veranda was that it was shaded by a large, willowy tree. The next time I decided to serve dinner on our porch, we instead dined "on the veranda." That's when I came up with this menu.

*A Sunday
Evening Supper
on the Veranda*

--- *hints* ---

- The Grilled Eggplant and Goat Cheese can be made ahead and reheated before serving.

- The Basil Lentil Salad can be made in advance as can the chutney.

- You can purchase praline powder, but crushing real pralines gives a spectacular texture to the raspberry cream.

# m • e • n • u

Grilled Eggplant and Goat Cheese

Basil Lentil Salad

Shrimp Studded Potato Pancakes

Shallot Sesame Sour Cream Chutney

Pecan Praline Raspberry Cream

## Grilled Eggplant and Goat Cheese

*To grill eggplant:*

1 large eggplant

1 tablespoon fresh minced garlic

2 tablespoons olive oil

1 teaspoon soy sauce

Cut eggplant into 8 1-inch rounds. Place in zipper lock bag with garlic, oil, and soy sauce and shake. Grill over medium-hot coals for 2 minutes per side. Remove to ovenproof tray.

*To assemble:*

8 ounces fresh goat cheese

1/8 cup extra virgin olive oil

1 tablespoon fresh minced garlic

1/4 cup fresh chopped parsley

Divide goat cheese among slices of eggplant. Mix together oil, garlic, and parsley and drizzle over cheese. Broil about 2 minutes until cheese melts and begins to brown.

Serves 6–8.

A Sunday
Evening Supper
on the Veranda

—— *words of* ——
*appreciation*

*Our friends are rare in life, and for those we have, we are blessed. To cherish one's friend is to cherish one's own heart, as that is where a friend should always be.*

# Basil Lentil Salad

1 1/2 cups lentils

1 tablespoon extra virgin olive oil

1 tablespoon fresh minced garlic

1 cup chopped white onion

1 cup fresh chopped red bell pepper

1/2 cup celery

1/2 cup fresh minced parsley

1 teaspoon dried oregano

3 cups water

salt and pepper to taste

2/3 cup fresh chopped basil leaves

Rinse and pick over lentils and set aside to drain. Heat oil in heavy saucepan over medium-high heat and stir in garlic and onion. Sauté for 5 minutes and stir in lentils, red pepper, celery, parsley, and oregano. Stir in water, and reduce heat to medium-low. Cover and simmer until lentils are tender and most of the liquid is absorbed. Remove from heat to cool. Season with salt and pepper and stir in basil.

Serves 6–8.

# Shrimp Studded Potato Pancakes

3 cups shredded potatoes

2/3 cup minced white onion

5 eggs, lightly beaten

salt and pepper to taste

2 pounds fresh cleaned small shrimp

safflower or canola oil for frying

Mix together the potato, onion, egg, salt, and pepper. Rinse the shrimp, pat dry, and mix into potato mixture.

Heat about 1/8-inch oil in a large, heavy sauté pan over medium-high heat, and place spoonfuls of the potato shrimp mixture in the hot oil. Fry about 5 to 7 minutes on each side or until golden brown. Pancakes may be held on tray in warm oven until all are cooked.

Makes about 10–12 pancakes.

# Shallot Sesame Sour Cream Chutney

1/4 cup sesame seeds

1 teaspoon safflower oil

1/2 cup fresh chopped shallots

1 tablespoon fresh minced garlic

1 1/2 cups sour cream

1 teaspoon paprika

salt and pepper to taste

In a heavy, nonstick sauté pan, toast sesame seeds over medium-high heat until they pop and begin to brown. Stir in oil, shallots, and garlic and sauté until shallots are golden brown. Cool and mix with sour cream and paprika. Season with salt and pepper. Cover and refrigerate until ready to use.

Serves 6–8.

 ## Pecan Praline Raspberry Cream

2 pints raspberries

1 cup granulated sugar

1 pint heavy whipping cream

1/4 cup powdered sugar

1 pound coarsely crushed pecan pralines

Rinse raspberries and place in heavy saucepan over medium heat and stir in sugar. Cook until mixture begins to simmer, and reduce heat. Simmer for 10 minutes. Remove to bowl, cover, and refrigerate until very cold. Whip cream with electric mixer, and slowly add powdered sugar. Beat until stiff peaks are formed and stir in raspberry sauce. Divide pralines among 6 or 8 serving dishes or champagne glasses, and spoon raspberry cream over the praline.

Serves 6–8.

# An Italian Style Vegetarian Feast

A lot of our friends are vegetarians, and I am always challenged to create a meal they find memorable. This roasted pepper lasagna à la vodka is something to crave, and if you must have meat with your meal, it makes a wonderful side dish. I was doing a fund-raiser with a group of friends and decided to make a planning meeting over lunch with the lasagna and a salad. I received applause for the selection. Zabaglione is an important dessert in anyone's recipe file. It is quick, easy, delicious, and made from ingredients that one usually has on hand.

# chef harry & friends

## An Italian Style Vegetarian Feast

### — hints —

- The pate and vinaigrette can be made a day or two ahead.
- The lasagna can be assembled the day before and baked before serving.
- The Citrus Zabaglione can also be made in advance and served cold, but I think it is best when served right from the stove.

# m・e・n・u

### Pate of Mediterranean Olives, Capers, and Garlic

### Toasted Garlic Vinaigrette with Mixed Italian Greens

### Grilled Portobellos

### Roasted Pepper Lasagna à la Vodka

### Citrus Zabaglione

## Pate of Mediterranean Olives, Capers, and Garlic

1 16-ounce jar Calamata olives, drained and pitted

1/4 cup capers, drained

2 tablespoons fresh minced garlic

Place ingredients in bowl of food processor fitted with steel blade and process until smooth. Serve room temperature with crusty bread.

Makes about 1 cup.

## Toasted Garlic Vinaigrette with Mixed Italian Greens

1/4 cup extra virgin olive oil

1/4 cup fresh thinly sliced garlic

1/2 cup balsamic vinegar

1 tablespoon dried oregano

2 tablespoons granulated sugar

salt and pepper to taste

1 cup grated Parmesan cheese

12 to 14 ounces fresh Italian salad greens

Heat oil in a small pan over medium-high heat and stir in garlic. Cook until garlic is golden brown. Remove from heat and cool. Stir together oil, garlic, vinegar, oregano, sugar, salt, and pepper. Toss dressing with cheese and greens.

Serves 6–8

An Italian Style
Vegetarian Feast

—— *words of* ——
*appreciation*

*Being together around the table, friends and family, we are able to appreciate the most important things in life. May our blessings continue and bring us together again soon.*

**An Italian Style
Vegetarian Feast**

 Grilled Portobellos

1 1/2 pounds portobello mushrooms

3 tablespoons extra virgin olive oil

1 teaspoon fresh minced garlic

salt and fresh cracked pepper to taste

Trim and rinse mushrooms and pat dry. Mix together oil, garlic, salt, and pepper, and marinate mushrooms up to 2 hours. Grill over medium-hot coals until tender, about 2 minutes per side. Slice.

Serves 6–8.

 Roasted Pepper Lasagna
à la Vodka

*For the sauce:*

1 tablespoon extra virgin olive oil

1 cup fresh chopped onion

2 tablespoons fresh minced garlic

1 tablespoon dried or 3 tablespoons fresh minced basil

1 teaspoon dried or 1 tablespoon fresh minced oregano

salt and pepper to taste

32 ounces pureed or strained tomatoes

1 tablespoon granulated sugar

1 cup heavy cream

1/4 cup vodka

2 tablespoons butter

1/2 cup shredded Parmesan cheese

2 cups roasted red peppers, sliced

Heat the oil in a large, heavy saucepan over medium-high heat and stir in the onions and garlic. Sauté to just brown, and reduce heat to medium. Stir in basil and oregano and cook for 1 minute. Season with salt and pepper and stir in tomatoes and sugar. Reduce heat to simmer sauce for 30 minutes. Stir in cream, vodka, butter, and cheese until creamy. Remove from heat. Stir in red peppers.

*To make the lasagna:*

12 cooked lasagna noodles (you may use the 'no precook required' kind, too)

2 cups ricotta cheese, seasoned with salt and pepper to taste

2 cups shredded mozzarella cheese

1 cup shredded Parmesan cheese

In an ungreased 9 x 13-inch lasagna pan, place about 1 cup of the sauce in the bottom. Place a layer of noodles over that. Spoon another cup of sauce over the noodles, and spread 1/2 of the ricotta over that. Spoon another cup of sauce over the ricotta, and sprinkle 1/2 cup of the mozzarella over that. Repeat with another layer. Finish with a third layer of noodles and the balance of the sauce. Sprinkle the rest of the mozzarella over the top, and sprinkle the Parmesan over that. Bake in preheated 325 degree oven until bubbly and brown, about 50 minutes. Allow to sit 5 minutes before cutting.

Serves 8–10.

# Citrus Zabaglione

| | |
|---|---|
| 4–6 cups assorted fruit and berries | zest from 2 lemons |
| 1½ cups sugar | zest from 1 orange |
| 2 cups concord grape wine | 6 egg yolks, slightly beaten |

Cut up fresh fruit and berries. Arrange fruit and berries in serving dishes. In a zabaglione bowl or saucepan sitting over a pan of simmering water, stir the sugar as you gradually add the wine. Stir in the zests. As the liquid begins to warm, stir in the egg yolks and whisk constantly until mixture changes color and thickens like a light custard, about 12-15 minutes. Spoon over fruit and serve.

Makes enough for 8 servings.

# All Aboard with Gary Coleman

*Gary Coleman is a funny man, and we hit it off instantly. He is kind and caring, and my daughter is crazy about him. In spite of his fame, he is quite down to earth and a reflection of his midwestern upbringing. We never think of him as a celebrity when we hang around together. One day we were booked to go to the same event in San Francisco, and he and a few others and I met at the airport. We were flying an airline without a VIP lounge, and it was then that I realized how popular Gary is. It was almost scary to watch the people, from two to ninety, run up and want his autograph.*

Now, whenever we are in a crowd and he is trying not to be recognized with his baseball cap pulled down over his face, I like to drop back a few steps, point to him, and say loudly: "Hey, isn't that Gary Coleman right there? Hey, man, that's Gary Coleman!"

It really drives him nuts and creates a minor stampede. If we are waiting for something, a path is usually created, which I stroll down to wait at the destination for him as he draws the crowd. When I do something like that, I know I had better make him one of his favorite meals. And there are few things Gary likes better than my Crab Cakes with Red Peppers and Turkey Chili!

— *hints* —

- The crab cakes can be made early in the day and reheated in a sauté pan or the oven.

- The dipping sauce and cilantro butter can be made the day before, as can the chili.

- The chili recipe makes a ton, but you will want to eat it over a couple of days and freeze some for later. It makes great nachos for a party!

- I like this corn bread right out of the oven, but it, like the apple crumble, can be made earlier in the day and reheated.

# m · e · n · u

Crab Cakes with Red Peppers

Curried Lemon Dipping Sauce

Turkey Chili

Jalapeno Corn Bread

Cilantro Chili Butter

Orange Apple Crumble

## Crab Cakes with Red Peppers

1 pound fresh lump crab meat,
   rinsed and picked over for shell

1/2 cup minced white onion

1/2 cup minced bell pepper

2 tablespoons fresh minced garlic

1/4 cup sweet pickle relish

1/2 cup mayonnaise

4 eggs

salt and pepper to taste

1 dash Worcestershire sauce

2/3 cup bread crumbs

butter for frying

Mix together all of the ingredients in a bowl. Heat 2 tablespoons butter in a large, heavy, nonstick sauté pan. Form small patties from the crab mixture, about 2 bites each, and fry in the butter to brown on both sides. Remove to oven-proof tray, and hold finished crab cakes in oven while frying balance, using additional butter as needed.

Makes about 30 small cakes.

## Curried Lemon Dipping Sauce

1 cup mayonnaise

2 tablespoons yellow mustard

juice from 1 lemon

zest from 1 lemon

1 tablespoon sweet curry blend

Tabasco sauce to taste

1 finely chopped or grated hard boiled egg (optional)

cracked pepper to taste

All Aboard with
Gary Coleman

—— words of ——
appreciation

*Making new friends as we
walk down life's path is
often a result of chance.
Being a friend is an art
that is improved over
a lifetime.*

Mix all ingredients together. Cover and refrigerate until ready to serve.

Makes almost 2 cups.

## Turkey Chili

1 tablespoon extra virgin olive oil

2 chopped white onions

3 tablespoons fresh minced garlic

2 pounds ground turkey

2 teaspoons salt

3 chopped bell peppers

30 ounces prepared black beans

30 ounces prepared kidney beans

30 ounces red beans

130 ounces crushed tomatoes

3 tablespoons ground cumin or to taste

2 tablespoons mild chili powder or to taste

2 tablespoons paprika

1/4 cup granulated sugar

grated cheddar cheese, chopped onion, and jalapeno slices for garnish

Heat oil in large pot over medium-high heat and stir in onion and garlic. Sauté 5 minutes and stir in turkey. Sauté until turkey is browned and well-done. Add salt and sauté 1 minute more. Stir in bell pepper and sauté 2 minutes more. Stir in beans and tomatoes and season with cumin, chili powder, paprika, and sugar. Simmer 2 hours, reseason, and serve or cover, refrigerate, and serve the next day (it is really better if it sits overnight). It freezes well, and an attractive large jar full with a basket of chips is a great appetizer to bring to a party…just heat and serve.

Makes a huge pot of chili.

 ## Jalapeno Corn Bread

1 ½ cups corn meal

1 ½ cups unbleached all purpose flour

1 tablespoon baking powder

1 teaspoon salt

4 eggs, lightly beaten

1 ½ cups milk

1 ½ cups shredded cheddar cheese

1 stick butter

1 cup minced white or yellow onion

1/4 cup fresh sliced jalapeno rounds (Wear rubber gloves
    when handling hot peppers.)

Mix together the meal, flour, powder, and salt. Mix together the eggs and the milk, and stir them into the dry ingredients to mix well. Blend for 1 minute and stir in cheese. In a 9 x 13-inch baking pan, melt the butter in a preheated 375 degree oven, and when just melted, stir in the onion and jalapeno. Return to oven, and watch for onion to begin to brown, about 5 minutes. The pan should be hot! Pour the batter into the hot pan, and reduce oven heat to 340 degrees. Bake until top puffs up and springs back when gently pressed. Bread should also brown on top. Turn out bread and cut into pieces with onion, jalapeno "crust" on top.

Serves 4–6.

 Cilantro Chili Butter

1 stick butter, softened to room temperature
1/4 cup fresh chopped cilantro leaves
1 teaspoon sweet chili pepper
1/2 teaspoon salt

Mix ingredients together to blend. Serve with jalapeno corn bread or cover and refrigerate until ready to serve. Bring to room temperature before serving.

Makes about 1/3 cup.

 Orange Apple Crumble

*For the apples:*
7 Granny Smith or other tart apples
juice from 1 orange
1 cup powdered sugar
1/3 cup flour
1 teaspoon cinnamon

*For the topping:*

1 stick butter, cut into pieces

1 cup oatmeal

1 cup unbleached all purpose four

2 cups brown sugar

1 cup white sugar

zest from 1 orange

Core and slice the apples and toss with orange juice, powdered sugar, 1/3 cup flour, and cinnamon. Place in a well-buttered baking dish to accommodate (a deep lasagna pan works great). Place topping ingredients in food processor fitted with steel blade and pulse until the texture of coarse meal. Place in an even layer over the apples and bake in a preheated 350 degree oven until top is brown and apples are bubbly. Serve warm with vanilla ice cream.

Serves 8–12.

# Maine Coast Respite

If you haven't been to Maine's bold coast, I highly recommend it. September in Maine with the leaves changing color along the coast is truly something to behold. The crashing surf, the mountains, the islands, the sunrises and sunsets; Maine is a special place. Then, there is the food. Incredible organic produce is everywhere and very inexpensive. The meals served in the restaurants, even the simple ones, are fresh and delicious. There are places along coastal roads to enjoy whole steamed lobsters and exceptional homebaked pies and cakes. It is an inspiration, not only to eat in Maine but to cook there as well. This menu is full of some of our favorite Downeast creations.

*Maine Coast
Respite*

- The bread and butter pickles can be made several days ahead.
- The pasta for the salad can be cooked until al dente, cooled under cold water, tossed with a dash of oil, covered, and held a day in advance. This gets a big step out of the way.
- Use only fresh crab.
- You can make any delicious tea and add a little honey to it before refrigerating.

# m · e · n · u

Quick Maine Bread and Butter Pickles

Coastal Crab Roll

Bold Coast Pasta Salad

Pick Your Own Blueberry Crisp

Lupine Honey Bee Tea

## Quick Maine Bread and Butter Pickles

1 cup water

1 cup sugar

1/8 cup red wine vinegar

1 onion, sliced into bite-sized slices

2 tablespoons yellow mustard seed

1 16-ounce jar refrigerated, kosher dill pickles, drained and sliced

In a heavy saucepan over medium heat, stir together water, sugar, and vinegar and bring to low boil. Boil for 5 minutes. Stir in onion and mustard seed and boil 2 minutes more. Remove from heat and stir in dill pickle slices. Allow to sit overnight or up to 4 days in the refrigerator, covered.

Serves 8–12.

 ## Coastal Crab Roll

1½ cups mayonnaise

1/2 cup chopped sweet gherkins

1 tablespoon yellow mustard

1½ to 2 pounds fresh cooked crab meat, rinsed and picked over
   for shell

6 to 8 French style rolls

shredded red lettuce for sandwiches, rinsed and patted dry

Mix together the mayonnaise, gherkins, and yellow mustard. Toss in crab to coat. Divide among split rolls and top with lettuce. Serve immediately.

Serves 6–8.

—— *words of* ——
*appreciation*

*Nature is bold and beautiful, warm and freezing, wet and dry. We are so blessed to be part of this wonderful world and give thanks for being together to share in it.*

Bold Coast Pasta Salad

1 pound dry pasta, a cut shape works best for salad

salted water for cooking pasta

2/3 cup extra virgin olive oil

2/3 cup red wine vinegar

1 tablespoon dried oregano

1/2 cup fresh chopped basil leaves

2 tablespoons fresh minced garlic

3 tablespoons granulated sugar

salt and pepper to taste

2 cups fresh blanched or frozen mixed peas

2 cups corn kernels, frozen, thawed, or canned, rinsed and drained

2 cups chopped seeded tomato

1 red onion, chopped

Cook the pasta until al dente, drain, and rinse under cold water. Mix together the oil, vinegar, oregano, basil, garlic, sugar, salt, and pepper. Toss with pasta and add balance of ingredients. Toss again and reseason if needed.

Serves 8–10.

 Pick Your Own Blueberry Crisp

6 cups fresh blueberries, rinsed and picked over

1 cup powdered sugar

1¼ cups unbleached all purpose flour

1 stick butter, cut into pieces

1 cup oatmeal

2 cups brown sugar

1 cup white sugar

2 tablespoons maple syrup

1 teaspoon ground cinnamon

Toss the blueberries with the powdered sugar and 1/4 cup flour. Place in buttered baking dish or casserole. Place butter, oatmeal, 1 cup flour, brown sugar, white sugar, maple syrup, and cinnamon in food processor and process until texture of coarse meal. Place in a layer over the berries and bake in preheated 350 degree oven until top browns and blueberries bubble, about 40 minutes.

Serves 8.

 ## Lupine Honey Bee Tea

1/2 gallon spring water

6 fruity tea bags (raspberry or peach cinnamon, for example)

1 cinnamon stick

2 sprigs fresh mint, rinsed

1/4 cup lupine honey (or any good quality honey)

Bring water to boil. Remove from heat and stir in balance of ingredients. Allow to sit for 20 minutes. Remove tea bags, cinnamon, and mint. Refrigerate and serve over ice.

Makes 1/2 gallon.

# A Legendary Meal for Legend Terry Moore

*When I arrived at Terry Moore's, she greeted me with that gorgeous smile and her hair in curlers. Wrapped in a lounging robe, she was as sexy as could be, curlers and all. She seemed thrilled to have a man in the kitchen, even though her own man likes to cook for her, too. Her kitchen was full of memorabilia from her more than sixty films, and I was thrilled to be cooking in the middle of motion picture history.*

She inspired me, and the meal ended up being sensational. I had unknowingly picked her favorite flowers for the table, and we had lots of votive candles and beautiful things. She had asked a friend to come by and play the piano, and one of her friends, songwriter Carol Connors entertained us along with the pianist. It was wonderful. Every time I run into actor Dennis Cole, another guest at Terry's, he always asks, "Hey Harry, do you have any of those lamb chops with you?" He knows how to make a chef feel good!

A Legendary
Meal for
Legend Terry
Moore

— *hints* —

- The dipping sauce, salad dressing, and glaze for the hens can be made a day in advance.

- The rice and apple cake can be made early in the day and reheated before serving.

- Purchase your pre-cooked cocktail shrimp at a market where they will do it to order. They should be as good as if you did it yourself.

# m • e • n • u

Tiny Marinated Grilled Lamb Chops

Apricot Mint Dipping Sauce

Shrimp and Fresh Dill in Ouzo

Chopped Caesar Salad

Glazed Cornish Hens

Rice with Cranberries

Dutch Apple Cake

## Tiny Marinated Grilled Lamb Chops

24 baby lamb chops
1/8 cup olive oil
2 tablespoons fresh minced garlic
1 tablespoon dried oregano
1/8 cup soy sauce
1 teaspoon fresh cracked pepper
kosher salt

Have the butcher clean the bone nicely, and make sure these are beautiful because they will not be inexpensive. Mix together the oil, garlic, oregano, soy sauce, and pepper. Marinate lamb chops 2 hours or overnight. Cover the bones of the chops before grilling. Grill chops over hot coals until seared and charred on the outside and pink on the inside, about 2 minutes per side. Sprinkle with salt if desired. Remove foil and serve.

Serves 8 as an appetizer.

## Apricot Mint Dipping Sauce

1 teaspoon extra virgin olive oil
1/4 cup minced shallots
1 pound dried apricots, chopped
1 cup water

20 ounces apricot all fruit preserves
juice from 2 lemons
rind from 2 lemons, chopped
1 cup fresh mint leaves, chopped

Heat olive oil in a heavy saucepan over medium-high heat. Stir in the shallots and saute until browned. Stir in the apricots

—— *words of* ——
*appreciation*

*Sometimes, when looking about, it is hard not to be overcome by our surroundings. We have been blessed with beautiful lives, beautiful friends, and a world of wonder. We toast to long life and good health!*

and water. Reduce heat to medium and stir in preserves and lemon juice. Bring to a simmer, and reduce heat. Add lemon rind and simmer for 10 minutes. Stir in mint and allow to cool. Cover and refrigerate until ready to use.

Makes about 2 cups.

##  Shrimp and Fresh Dill in Ouzo

1 1/2 pounds freshly cooked, cleaned cocktail shrimp

12 ounces marinated Sun Dried tomatoes, drained

1 cup chopped celery

1/4 cup chopped dill weed

juice from 1 lemon

1 cup Ouzo

cracked pepper to taste

Toss everything together, cover, and refrigerate up to 36 hours before serving.

Serves 10–12.

##  Chopped Caesar Salad

juice from 3 lemons

12 anchovy filets

8 cloves garlic

1 teaspoon Worcestershire sauce

1 teaspoon cracked pepper

1 cup grated Parmesan cheese

1 cup extra virgin olive oil

1 fresh cucumber, chopped

2 firm tomatoes, seeded and chopped

2 heads Belgian endive, chopped

2 heads radicchio, chopped

1 romaine heart, chopped

1 bunch scallions, chopped

1 cup black olives, chopped

1/4 lb. shaved Parmesan cheese

Place the lemon juice, anchovies, garlic, Worcestershire, pepper, and Parmesan in the bowl of a food processor fitted with steel blade and process until blended. Gradually add oil in a stream and process until thick. Toss together cucumber, tomatoes, endive, radicchio, romaine, scallions, and olives with dressing. Top with shaved Parmesan.

Serves 8.

##  Glazed Cornish Hens

8 Cornish hens

1/2 cup extra virgin olive oil

1/4 cup fresh minced garlic

1 tablespoon salt

1 teaspoon fresh cracked pepper

1 tablespoon canola oil

1 minced onion

16 ounces orange marmalade

A Legendary
Meal for
Legend Terry
Moore

Rinse the hens and pat dry. Mix together the olive oil, garlic, salt, and fresh cracked pepper. Paint the hens with the mixture and allow to stand for 30 minutes. Heat the canola oil in a saucepan over medium-high heat, and toast the onion until brown. Turn down heat to low and stir in marmalade. Keep over warm flame.

Either grill the hens over hot coals on covered grill for 15 minutes or sear in oven on highest setting for 15 minutes. Remove from heat source, and baste hens with marmalade mixture. Roast hens in preheated 325 degree oven until done, about 60 minutes, basting with glaze as they roast.

Serves 8.

─── *serving* ───
*suggestions*

Hollow out orange cups made from fresh oranges with edges that have been scalloped. Spoon rice into orange cups and serve. (With remaining orange pulp, remove seeds and place in blender with 2 cups of ice and 1 cup vodka. A frozen screwdriver is born!)

 ## Rice with Cranberries

1 stick unsalted butter

2 tablespoons fresh minced garlic

1 cup fresh minced onion

2 cups wild rice or wild rice blend

4 cups water

1 tablespoon salt or to taste

1 cup dried cranberries

1 cup roasted and salted cashews

Heat butter in heavy saucepan over medium-high heat and stir in garlic and onion. Sauté for 5 minutes and stir in rice. Sauté for 1 minute and stir in water and salt. Bring to simmer, cover, and cook for 40 to 45 minutes or until tender and liquid is absorbed. Fluff with fork and toss in berries and cashews.

Serves 8–10.

# Dutch Apple Cake

*For the apples:*

1 cup toasted unsalted whole almonds in the skin

6 apples, cored and sliced

1 cup powdered sugar

1/4 cup unbleached all purpose flour

1 tablespoon cinnamon

1 tablespoon vanilla extract

*For the topping:*

1 stick butter, cut into pieces

1 cup unbleached all purpose flour

1 cup brown sugar

1 cup white sugar

1 cup slivered almonds

Place the whole almonds in a food processor fitted with a steel blade. Pulverize almonds and toss with apples, powdered sugar, 1/4 cup flour, cinnamon, and vanilla. Place in 9 or 10-inch false bottom cake pan.

Place topping ingredients in bowl of food processor (no need to wash after pulverizing nuts) and pulse until contents is texture of coarse meal. Pour over apples. Cover with foil and bake in pre-heated 325 degree oven for 60 minutes. Uncover and bake 30 to 40 minutes more, until topping is brown. Cool cake, and run a knife around the edge before unmolding carefully. Serve warm.

Serves 8–10.

# Asian Delight

If I had to pick a style of cuisine as my favorite, one I would have to cook and eat for the rest of my life, it would be Asian. The blends of flavors, textures, and methods make for limitless combinations and satisfactions. From dim sum in New York to Thai barbecue in Los Angeles, I never tire of the delights. We have had some great times with friends cooking Asian food all afternoon, eating all evening, and talking until late at night. "Dim sum" means food for the heart. I find Asian cuisine food for the soul.

# m . e . n . u

Chicken Nam Sod

Pan Fried Dumplings

Sesame Scallion Dipping Sauce

Szechwan Green Beans

Home Style Beef with Peanuts

Mandarin Pineapple Upside Down Cake

--- *hints* ---

- The Sesame Scallion Dipping Sauce can be made a day or two in advance.

- The cake can be made early in the day and served room temperature or rewarmed.

- Nam sod can be made a day in advance and assembled before serving.

- The dumplings can be assembled a day in advance and cooked before serving.

# Chicken Nam Sod

2 tablespoons safflower oil

3/4 cup pine nuts

1 pound ground chicken

3 tablespoons fresh minced garlic

3 tablespoons fresh minced ginger

1 tablespoon soy sauce

1/4 cup fresh minced cilantro

8 ounces Hoisin sauce

1/2 teaspoon sesame oil

24 to 30 Belgian endive leaves, trimmed, rinsed, and patted dry

Heat 1 tablespoon of safflower oil in large, heavy, nonstick sauté pan over medium-high flame. Add pine nuts and toast, stirring frequently, until golden brown. Remove from pan and reserve. Heat remaining tablespoon of oil in same pan, without washing, over medium-high heat, and sauté chicken until browned and dry. Stir in garlic, ginger, and soy sauce and sauté 2 minutes more. Remove from heat and stir in cilantro, Hoisin, and sesame oil. Cool. Divide among endive leaves.

Serves 8–10 as an appetizer.

—words of—
appreciation

*Words from the wise teach only those who will listen.*

# Pan Fried Dumplings

1 medium head Savoy cabbage, trimmed, rinsed, and chopped

2 medium carrots, peeled and cut into chunks

1/4 cup fresh minced ginger

1/8 cup fresh minced garlic

1 teaspoon soy sauce

3 egg whites, slightly beaten

1 teaspoon corn starch

24 won ton skins

2 teaspoons safflower oil

1 cup chicken or vegetable stock

Place cabbage in food processor fitted with steel blade and pulse to mince finely. Place cabbage in strainer and press out excess moisture. Place cabbage in mixing bowl. Mince carrots in processor and pulse in ginger and garlic. Mix soy, about 2 of the 3 egg whites, and cornstarch into cabbage. Mix well.

Using a cornstarch dusted surface to work on, place a mound of the filling in the center of each won ton skin, paint edges of skins with remaining egg white, and gather edges around filling to form pouches. Heat 1 teaspoon oil over medium-high heat in heavy, nonstick sauté pan, and arrange 12 of the dumplings in the hot oil. Brown the bottoms, and reduce heat to medium. Pour 1/2 of the broth over the dumplings and cover tightly, steaming for 12 minutes. Repeat with other dumplings, holding first batch in warm oven.

Serves 1–12.

## Sesame Scallion Dipping Sauce

1/4 cup seasoned rice vinegar

1/8 cup soy sauce

1 tablespoon sesame oil

2 minced scallions

1 teaspoon fresh minced garlic

1 teaspoon fresh minced ginger

Combine ingredients and keep in covered container in the refrigerator until ready to dip. Great for dumplings, spring roll, nam sod, grilled chicken, meat, or fish.

Makes about 1/2 cup.

 ## Szechwan Green Beans

2 pounds string beans, trimmed and rinsed

2 tablespoons canola or safflower oil

2 tablespoons water

1 cup chopped scallions

1/2 cup minced water chestnuts

1/8 cup fresh minced ginger

2 tablespoons fresh minced garlic

1 teaspoon corn starch

1/2 cup chicken or vegetable stock

1/8 cup sherry

2 tablespoons soy sauce

Thoroughly dry the green beans (placing the beans on paper towel and giving them a couple minutes with a hair dryer works great and will prevent spattering later in the hot oil) and heat oil in a large, nonstick pot or wok with lid. Place beans into hot oil and stir fry 1 minute. Holding lid in one hand, quickly and carefully add water to pan, and quickly cover pan to avoid a burn. Steam beans for 6 minutes or until tender and skins blister.

Stir in scallions, water chestnuts, ginger, and garlic. Mix corn starch with stock, sherry, and soy sauce and stir into beans. Stir fry until sauce thickens, about 2 or 3 minutes.

Serves 6–8.

 ## Home Style Beef with Peanuts

2 pounds flank steak

1/2 cup dry sherry

1/4 cup soy sauce

1 tablespoon safflower or canola oil

4 egg whites, lightly beaten

1/8 cup plus 1 tablespoon corn starch

salted boiling water

1 tablespoon peanut oil

2 tablespoons fresh minced garlic

2 tablespoons fresh minced ginger

1 cup chopped red bell pepper

1 cup fresh shredded carrot

1 cup fresh chopped scallion

1 cup chicken stock

1/2 cup Hoisin sauce

1/2 cup red chili paste

1 cup dry roasted salted peanuts

Place beef in freezer until almost frozen but not solid, about 2 hours. Shred beef with sharp knife or in food processor fitted with shredding blade. Toss beef with 1/4 cup sherry, 1/8 cup soy, safflower oil, and egg whites. Mix well. Sprinkle 1/8 cup cornstarch over beef and mix again. Cover and refrigerate up to 24 hours. Bring meat to room temperature and boil in large pot of salted boiling water about 6 minutes after water returns to boil again. Drain.

Heat peanut oil in wok over high heat and stir in garlic and ginger. Stir fry for 1 minute, and add bell pepper and carrot. Stir fry 2 minutes more and stir in scallions. Stir a little of the stock into the cornstarch to dissolve, and add balance of stock and slowly stir in to wok. Stir fry 2 minutes more. Stir in Hoisin and chili paste and stir fry 1 minute more. Stir in beef and cook for 2 minutes. Stir in peanuts and serve.

Serves 6–8 and is smashing over crispy rice noodles or fresh bean sprouts.

# Mandarin Pineapple Upside Down Cake

*For the topping:*
2 sticks unsalted butter
2 cups brown sugar
1/2 teaspoon vanilla
1/2 cup milk
1 ripe pineapple trimmed, cored, and cut into small chunks
11 ounces mandarin oranges, drained, liquid reserved

## Asian Delight

For the cake:

2 cups granulated sugar

liquid from mandarin oranges plus orange juice to make 1 cup

2/3 cup safflower oil

5 eggs

3 cups unbleached all purpose flour

1 teaspoon baking powder

——— caution ———

Caramel is hot! Place plate over cake and turn over quickly and carefully. Use a towel as an extra precaution. Serve warm, if possible.

Make the topping by melting the butter and the brown sugar in a heavy saucepan over medium heat and stirring in the vanilla and milk. Heat until sugar is dissolved, and pour mixture into deep 9 x 14-inch buttered baking pan. Arrange pineapple and oranges over mixture.

Beat together the sugar, orange liquid, safflower oil, and eggs until pale. Blend in flour and baking powder and beat for 1 minute. Pour mixture over pineapple and oranges and bake in preheated 350 degree oven until cake is domed up in the center and browning, about 55 minutes.

Remove from oven and allow to stand 5 minutes before turning onto serving platter.

Serves 8–12.

# Italian Love Fest with Renee Taylor and Joseph Bologna

*Planning supper with Renee Taylor and Joe Bologna was an event in itself. In their stunning Beverly Hills manse, we all kept adding courses and suggesting things that sounded too good to leave out. The antipasto alone was a meal, as was pretty much every other individual course. But, no matter, as food is love, we wanted lots and lots of love!*

We really had fun, and there was enough food for an army. We were also taping my public television show that night and had enough to feed the entire crew, who did manage to polish off most everything. (A good crew can out eat any army.) I knew that I had made good food when my phone rang the next morning with Renee on the phone asking, "So dahling, where are the leftovers?!?"

*Italian Love
Fest with Renee
Taylor and
Joseph Bologna*

---
*h i n t s*
---

- This is a very aggressive menu in its entirety only because there are so many things to make.

- Nothing involved is too tough, though. You may want to omit the pasta, which is a tad rich, or the antipasto, or both.

- Most of the elements for the antipasto can be made in advance, and the polenta and torte can be made a day before.

- The Seafood Scampi also makes a great first course served over pasta or an olive crostini.

# m • e • n • u

## Grand Antipasto
(Marinated Asiago, Prosciutto Wrapped Figs, Mozzarella with Pesto, Mozzarella with Sun Dried Tomato, Genoa Marinated Shrimp, Grilled Calamari, Grilled Tomatoes and Parmesan, Grilled Marinated Peppers, and Grilled Scallions)

## Angel Hair Pasta with Garlic Crusted Sardines and Toasted Almond Crumbs

## Arugula and Radicchio with Toasted Pistachio Gorgonzola Vinaigrette

## Seafood Scampi

## Roasted Pepper Polenta

## Chocolate Mascarpone Torte

# Grand Antipasto

 Marinated Asiago

1/4 cup extra virgin olive oil

2 tablespoons fresh minced garlic

1 pound Asiago cheese,
  shaved or sliced into pieces

fresh cracked pepper

Mix together olive oil and garlic and drizzle over cheese. Crack fresh pepper over the top. Serve with crusty bread or focaccia.

Serves 8–12 as an appetizer.

Prosciutto Wrapped Figs

12 fresh figs, cut in half

24 thin slices prosciutto ham

Hold fig half in one hand, and wrap 1 slice of ham around it. Repeat with balance of figs and arrange attractively on tray. Voila, you're a caterer!

Serves 8–12 as an appetizer.

Mozzarella with Pesto

1 cup pine nuts

2 tablespoons fresh minced garlic

1 cup fresh basil leaves

1 tablespoon red wine vinegar

1 tablespoon extra virgin olive oil

salt and pepper to taste

2 large pieces fresh mozzarella
  cheese

—— words of ——
a p p r e c i a t i o n

*The richness that life holds is vast. Sharing in it while doing what we enjoy is a rare and precious blessing. How fortunate we are to be together sharing the rich gift of life!*

In a nonstick sauté pan over medium heat, toast pine nuts until golden. Stir in garlic. Remove from heat and cool. Combine in food processor with basil, red wine vinegar, olive oil, salt, and pepper and pulse until smooth. With a fine dental floss tightly pulled between hands, slice cheese into rounds. Arrange on platter, and divide pesto on top of cheese.

Makes about 12–16 pieces.

## Mozzarella with Sun Dried Tomato

12 ounces marinated Sun Dried tomatoes, drained
2 tablespoons fresh garlic
1 teaspoon dried oregano
2 large pieces fresh mozzarella cheese
fresh cracked pepper
fresh minced onion and parsley for garnish

Place the tomatoes, garlic, and oregano in the bowl of a food processor fitted with a steel blade. Puree. With a fine dental floss tightly pulled between hands, slice cheese into rounds. Arrange on platter, and divide tomato paste among tops of pieces. Crack fresh pepper over the top and sprinkle with minced onion and parsley.

Serves 8–12 as an appetizer.

## Genoa Marinated Shrimp

1/3 cup extra virgin olive oil

1 tablespoon fresh minced garlic

1 teaspoon dried oregano

1 pound, 24 to 30, cooked cocktail shrimp

24 to 30 thin slices Genoa salami

Mix together the oil, garlic, and oregano and toss with shrimp. Allow to marinate over night. Drain shrimp, and wrap each shrimp in a slice of Genoa, fastening with a toothpick to secure.

Serves 8–12 as an appetizer.

 ## Grilled Calamari

1/3 cup extra virgin olive oil

1 tablespoon fresh minced garlic

1 teaspoon soy sauce

fresh cracked pepper to taste

1 pound fresh cleaned calamari

Mix together the oil, garlic, and soy sauce and season with pepper. Toss with calamari, marinate up to 1 hour, and grill over medium-hot coals until done, about 3 to 4 minutes per side. Cut into pieces and serve room temperature.

Serves 8–12 as an appetizer.

*Italian Love*
*Fest with Renee*
*Taylor and*
*Joseph Bologna*

# Grilled Tomatoes and Parmesan

1/3 cup extra virgin olive oil

1 tablespoon fresh minced garlic

1 teaspoon soy sauce

fresh cracked pepper to taste

4 roma tomatoes or firm red tomatoes, cored and sliced into
   1/2-inch slices.

8 ounces shaved Parmesan

Mix together the olive oil, garlic, and soy and season with pepper. Drizzle over tomato slices, and grill tomato over medium-hot coals until tender, about 90 seconds per side. Arrange on serving platter and garnish with Parmesan.

Serves 8–12 as an appetizer.

# Grilled Marinated Peppers

1/3 cup extra virgin olive oil

1 tablespoon fresh minced garlic

1 teaspoon soy sauce

fresh cracked pepper to taste

4 red bell peppers, seeded and trimmed, quartered

Mix together the olive oil, garlic, and soy and season with pepper. Toss with peppers and grill over medium-hot coals until tender and skin blisters, about 2 minutes per side.

Serves 8–12 as an appetizer.

 ## Grilled Scallions

1/3 cup extra virgin olive oil

1 tablespoon fresh minced garlic

1 teaspoon soy sauce

fresh cracked pepper to taste

3 bunches fresh scallions, trimmed and rinsed

Mix together the olive oil, garlic, and soy and season with pepper. Toss with scallions and grill over medium-hot coals until greens begin to wilt, about 90 seconds per side.

Serves 8–12 as an appetizer.

 ## Angel Hair Pasta with Garlic Crusted Sardines and Toasted Almond Crumbs

*For the crumbs:*

1 tablespoon extra virgin olive oil

2 cups whole almonds in the skin

2 tablespoons fresh minced garlic

2 cups grated Parmesan cheese

Heat the oil in a large, heavy, nonstick sauté pan over medium-high heat and stir in the almonds and garlic until toasted and smelling irresistible. Cool. Pulverize in a food processor and mix with cheese.

*Italian Love
Fest with Renee
Taylor and
Joseph Bologna*

*For the sardines:*

1 tablespoon extra virgin olive oil

3 tablespoons fresh minced garlic

12 ounces whole headless, fresh or prepared, sardine filets

cracked fresh pepper

In a large, heavy, nonstick sauté pan over medium-high heat, heat the oil. Sauté the garlic and spread uniformly over the pan. Arrange the sardines on the sautéing garlic (arrange in lines side by side for easier turning) and brown on both sides. Sprinkle with pepper. Remove from heat. Set aside 8 of the prettiest fillets for garnish.

*For the pasta:*

8 servings angel hair pasta

1 stick butter

2 tablespoons fresh minced garlic

Boil 8 servings of angel hair pasta until al dente and drain; set aside. Melt butter and garlic in pan used to boil pasta, and toss pasta back in. Add 2/3 of the topping mixture and the sardines (except those reserved for garnish) and toss to mix. The sardines will break apart. Serve on warm plates and top with sardine reserved for garnish and balance of crumbs.

Serves 8.

## Arugula and Radicchio with Toasted Pistachio Gorgonzola Vinaigrette

2 tablespoons extra virgin olive oil

2 tablespoons fresh minced garlic

1 cup shelled pistachio nuts

2/3 cup safflower oil

2/3 cup red wine vinegar

2 tablespoons granulated sugar

1/2 cup fresh minced basil leaves

1 cup crumbled Gorgonzola

1 tablespoon dried oregano

1/2 cup minced onion

salt and pepper to taste (the Gorgonzola is salty!)

12 ounces baby arugula, rinsed and drained

2 heads firm radicchio, trimmed and shredded

Heat the olive oil in a heavy, nonstick sauté pan and stir in garlic and pistachios. Toast nuts and remove from heat. Cool and stir in safflower oil, vinegar, sugar, oregano, basil, and onion. Stir in Gorgonzola and season with salt and pepper. Toss with salad.

Serves at least 8.

# Seafood Scampi

2 sticks butter

1/4 cup fresh minced garlic

1 tablespoon soy sauce

2 pounds large, fresh cleaned shrimp

4 lobster tails, split, out of the shell, cleaned, and cut into chunks

1 1/2 pounds fresh sea scallops, cut in half

1/2 cup fresh chopped parsley

1 lemon

salt and pepper to taste

Heat butter in large, heavy, nonstick sauté pan over medium-high heat and stir in garlic. When garlic turns golden, stir in soy sauce and seafood and sauté until just done, about 4 or 5 minutes.

Stir in parsley, squeeze in the juice from the lemon, and season with salt and pepper. Serve over roasted pepper polenta, if desired.

Serves 8–10.

# Roasted Pepper Polenta

1/2 cup butter

1 cup minced onion

1 tablespoon salt

1 tablespoon fresh cracked pepper

1 pound polenta

4 cups water

1 cup diced roasted red pepper (or you can snatch one of the grilled ones from the above antipasto!)

Heat the butter in a heavy saucepan over medium-high heat and stir in onion. Sauté until golden and season with salt and pepper. Stir in polenta and mix well. Stir in water, and when simmering, reduce heat and continue to cook and stir until mixture is a thick paste.

Stir in peppers. Spread into a 1-inch layer on greased cookie sheet. Cut into pieces and cool. Serve warm. You may chill the polenta and grill later or warm wrapped in foil in the oven.

Serves 8–10.

## Chocolate Mascarpone Torte

*For the crust:*
1/3 pound graham crackers, broken
6 ounces pecan halves
1 stick butter, cut into pieces
1/4 cup sugar
1/2 teaspoon cinnamon

Pulse graham crackers and pecans in food processor until texture of meal. Pulse in butter, sugar, and cinnamon until the texture of coarse meal. Press into bottom and sides of 14-inch fluted tart pan with false bottom.

*Italian Love
Fest with Renee
Taylor and
Joseph Bologna*

*For the filling:*

12 ounces mascarpone cheese

1/2 pound pulverized pecan pralines

8 ounces cream cheese

1 cup sour cream

2 cups granulated sugar

3 eggs

1/2 cup cocoa powder

1 teaspoon vanilla extract

In the same processor bowl from above and without washing, place mascarpone, praline, cream cheese, sour cream, and sugar and combine with long pulses until blended. Pulse in the eggs and then the cocoa and vanilla. Scrape bowl and pulse to blend. Pour into crust, and bake in preheated 325 degree oven until center domes completely, about 55 to 65 minutes. Cool and serve with sorbet, if desired.

Serves 8–10.

# The Perfect Shower

*I never need a reason to throw a party. I love to have people over and can never wait until the next time. But when someone is getting married or having a baby, now that is reason to party! I seize every opportunity to celebrate, and the following menu was created for one of our good friends who was having her first baby. She had a girl, and to this day, I wonder if it had something to do with my pasta.*

— *h i n t s* —

- The brie can be assembled and refrigerated or frozen before baking and serving.

- The vinaigrette and blonde brownies can be made the day before, as can the sauce for the pasta. This is a very easy menu.

# m • e • n • u

## Baked Brie in Filo

## Baby Greens with Crab and Toasted Almond Vinaigrette

## Pretty in Pink Pasta

## Blonde Brownies and Berries

## Baked Brie in Filo

6 sheets filo pastry, handled according to directions on box

1/4 cup melted butter

1 whole small (8 to 16 ounce) round brie

1 cup apricot preserves

1 cup smoked almonds

Place first sheet of filo on buttered baking tray and paint with butter. Place another sheet on top, paint with butter, and so on until all 6 sheets are used. Place brie in center of filo. Spread preserves over top of brie, and sprinkle almonds over that. Gather pastry, and form a pouch around brie, pressing together to seal in brie. Paint entire bundle with butter, and bake in preheated 350 degree oven until pastry is brown and flaky, about 35 minutes.

Serves 8–12.

 ## Baby Greens with Crab and Toasted Almond Vinaigrette

1 tablespoon safflower oil

2 tablespoons fresh minced garlic

1 cup slivered almonds

1/2 cup fresh chopped basil leaves

1/2 cup red wine vinegar

1 tablespoon granulated sugar or to taste

2/3 cup extra virgin olive oil

salt and pepper to taste

—— *words of* ——
*appreciation*

*How lucky we are to be
together sharing life's joy.
We are so thankful to be
together—living, laughing,
and loving while we celebrate
this happy time.*

16 to 20 ounces baby salad greens

1 pound cooked crab, rinsed and picked over for shell, drained

Heat safflower oil in heavy skillet over medium-high heat until hot. Stir in garlic and almonds and sauté while stirring until almonds begin to toast and turn golden. Remove from heat and allow to stand 10 minutes. Stir in basil, vinegar, sugar, olive oil, salt, and pepper. Taste, and adjust seasoning if necessary. Toss greens with dressing, reserving most of the almonds in the bottom of the pan. Place tossed salad on platter or divide among plates and top with crab. Garnish with reserved almonds.

Serves 8.

 Pretty in Pink Pasta

1 tablespoon extra virgin olive oil

1 tablespoon fresh minced garlic

4 cups tomato puree

1 tablespoon dried oregano

2 cups milk or heavy cream

1 cup shredded Parmesan cheese

1 teaspoon sugar

salt and pepper to taste

1 cup fresh chopped basil leaves

8 servings angel hair pasta

shaved Parmesan for garnish

Heat oil in large, heavy saucepan over medium-high heat and stir in garlic. Sauté garlic until it begins to turn golden. Reduce heat to medium and stir in tomato puree and oregano. Bring contents to simmer and stir in milk or cream, Parmesan, and sugar. When sauce barely simmers, season with salt and pepper and

keep warm but do not boil. Stir in basil. Boil pasta until al dente, drain, and toss with sauce. Garnish with cheese (and a little more fresh chopped basil, if desired).

Serves 8.

 ## Blonde Brownies and Berries

3/4 pound butter

1 1/2 pounds brown sugar

1 cup white sugar

1 teaspoon vanilla

5 large eggs

2 1/2 cups unbleached all purpose flour

1 teaspoon baking powder

1 pint fresh berries

Beat butter, sugars, vanilla, and eggs until blended. Beat in flour and baking powder for 1 minute. Place in buttered nonstick jelly roll pan and bake in preheated 350 degree oven until the brownies rise and fall in the middle, about 25 to 30 minutes. Gently shake the pan if help is needed falling.

Cool and cut into squares. Serve with fresh berries of choice.

Makes 24–30 brownies.

# Picnic on the "Almost" Lawn with Connie Stevens

*Connie Stevens, in spite of her femininely sexy image, is a powerhouse. Her company, Forever Spring, has made television shopping history. She has homes going up in more than one state, and her phone rings constantly. Her daughters are following in her footsteps, and when you put Connie and her offspring together, you get an energy combination you can feel.*

We decided to have a garden party at a new home she was building in Beverly Hills on top of one of the highest points you can find. As the date grew near, the builder failed to keep up with our social schedule, and the day of the party, with the trucks coming down the driveway with the tables and chairs, we realized we had no garden. We did not even have a lawn!

No problem. With some pink tablecloths and a run to the florist, in less than an hour we turned a construction zone into a charming "Forever Spring" luncheon. Some days we can amaze even ourselves, and that was one of those days!

*Picnic on the "Almost" Lawn with Connie Stevens*

——— h i n t s ———

- With the exception of mixing the drinks, this entire menu can be made ahead of time.
- Even the shrimp are great cold, using the glaze as a dip. This also makes a wonderful buffet selection.

# m • e • n • u

Grecian Finger Sandwiches

Corn Pepper Relish with Fresh Lemon Thyme

Pink Lentil Salad

Bocconcini and Mini Multi-Colored
Tomato Salad

Grilled Shrimp in Apricot Hoisin
Sesame Glaze

Fresh Figs and Organic Raspberries

Hazelnut White Chocolate Squares

Double Chocolate Brownies

Coconut Almond Butterscotch Meltaways

Chocolate Dipped Apricots

White Star Mimosas

Passion Fruit Blend

Iced Tea with Peach Ice Cubes

# Grecian Finger Sandwiches

30 ounces prepared garbanzo beans, drained

8 cloves fresh garlic

8 ounces anchovy filets, drained

juice from 2 lemons

1 teaspoon Worcestershire sauce

1/3 cup safflower oil

1 cup fat free yogurt

salt and pepper to taste

2 rectangular soft flatbreads (lavosh) about 11 x 20-inch (large
   tortillas work well, too)

2 cups fresh rinsed watercress leaves

Process the garbanzos with the garlic, anchovy, lemon juice, and
Worcestershire in a food processor fitted with steel blade. Pulse
in the safflower oil and the yogurt. Season with salt and pepper,
scrape bowl, and process until smooth. Spread onto one side of
breads, and sprinkle watercress over the top. Roll up like jelly rolls
and slice diagonally to serve.

Makes about 24 finger sandwiches.

# Corn Pepper Relish with Fresh Lemon Thyme

1 pound frozen corn kernels, rinsed under cold water to thaw,
   drained

2 red bell peppers, trimmed, seeded, rinsed, and minced

1 cup minced scallion

chef harry & friends

Picnic on the
"Almost" Lawn
with Connie
Stevens

—— words of ——
appreciation

*There are many places to feel
as though you are on top of
the world. Capturing that
feeling and storing it in your
soul can be a source of
strength from within.*

juice from 2 lemons

1/2 cup extra virgin olive oil

1 teaspoon sugar

salt and pepper to taste

1/3 cup fresh chopped lemon thyme leaves (regular fresh thyme is fine, too)

Mix together the corn, peppers, and scallion. Blend the lemon juice with the olive oil, sugar, salt, and pepper. Pour over corn and toss. Stir in lemon thyme just before serving.

Serves 8.

## Pink Lentil Salad

1 pound fresh pink lentils or 4 cups prepared lentils, drained

2 tablespoons fresh minced garlic

1 tablespoon dried oregano

2 tablespoons extra virgin olive oil

1/3 cup red wine vinegar

1/8 cup granulated sugar

8 ounces marinated Sun Dried tomatoes with marinade, tomatoes sliced into pieces

salt and pepper to taste

Mix together all ingredients. Season with salt and pepper. Cover and refrigerate up to 24 hours before serving. Serve at room temperature.

Serves 8.

## Bocconcini and Mini Multi-Colored Tomato Salad

1/4 cup extra virgin olive oil

1/4 cup balsamic vinegar

2 tablespoons fresh minced garlic

1 teaspoon salt or to taste

1 pint mini multi-colored tomatoes, rinsed, or 2 cups seeded firm
   ripe tomato, chunked

1 pound fresh bocconcini (mini balls of fresh mozzarella), cut in half
   or 1 pound fresh cut up mozzarella

1 cup fresh chopped basil leaves

Mix together oil, vinegar, garlic, and salt. Toss together tomatoes and cheese, and sprinkle basil over the top. Drizzle oil mixture over the top, toss gently to mix, and serve.

Serves 6–8.

## Grilled Shrimp in Apricot Hoisin Sesame Glaze

*For the glaze:*

1 tablespoon extra virgin olive oil

2 tablespoons fresh minced garlic

1/4 cup sesame seeds

1 tablespoon fresh minced ginger root

1 cup apricot preserves

8 ounces Hoisin sauce

*Picnic on the
"Almost" Lawn
with Connie
Stevens*

Heat oil in heavy saucepan over medium-high heat and sauté garlic, sesame seeds, and ginger for 2 minutes. Stir in apricot preserves and Hoisin. Reduce heat to medium. Bring to simmer, and reduce heat to keep warm.

*For the shrimp:*

2 pounds large fresh cleaned shrimp

2 tablespoons fresh minced garlic

1/8 cup soy sauce

2 tablespoons extra virgin olive oil

Toss shrimp with garlic, soy sauce, and oil. Marinate up to 4 hours. Skewer shrimp and grill over hot coals until just done, about 2 minutes per side. Remove shrimp from skewers to heat-proof bowl, and pour glaze over shrimp. Toss to coat. Serve warm or cold.

Serves 8 or up to 24 as an appetizer.

# Fresh Figs and Organic Raspberries

8 fresh figs, rinsed, trimmed, and quartered

1 pint fresh raspberries (organic if available)

2 tablespoons powdered sugar

1/8 cup Grand Marnier or brandy

Toss gently to combine. Allow to soak and serve as is or over sponge cake or pound cake.

Makes about 2¹/₂ cups.

## Hazelnut White Chocolate Squares

1 stick butter

1½ cups graham cracker crumbs

24 ounces white chocolate chips

1½ cups chopped hazelnuts

7 ounces shredded coconut

1 can sweetened condensed milk

Melt the butter in a glass baking dish and set in 350 degree oven. Remove from oven, and sprinkle crumbs in an even layer over the butter. Sprinkle 1/2 of the white chocolate chips over that, then the nuts, the rest of the chips, and then the coconut. Pour the milk in an even layer over the coconut and return to oven until coconut toasts, about 30 minutes. Cool, cut into squares.

Makes about 18 squares.

## Double Chocolate Brownies

3/4 pound butter

1½ pounds brown sugar

1 cup white sugar

1 teaspoon vanilla

2½ cups unbleached all purpose flour

1 teaspoon baking powder

1/2 cup cocoa powder

12 ounces chocolate chips

5 eggs

Beat butter, sugars, vanilla, and eggs until blended. Beat in flour, baking powder, and cocoa for 1 minute. Stir in chocolate chips. Place in buttered nonstick jelly roll pan and bake in preheated 350 degree oven until the brownies rise and fall in the middle, about 25 to 30 minutes. Gently shake the pan if help is needed falling. Cool and cut into squares.

Makes 24 squares.

## Coconut Almond Butterscotch Meltaways

1 stick butter

1½ cups graham cracker crumbs

12 ounces chocolate chips

1½ cups slivered almonds

12 ounces butterscotch chips

7 ounces shredded coconut

1 can sweetened condensed milk

Melt the butter in a glass baking dish and set in 350 degree oven. Remove from oven, and sprinkle crumbs in an even layer over the butter. Sprinkle the chocolate chips over that, then the nuts, then the butterscotch chips, and then the coconut. Pour the milk in an even layer over the coconut and return to oven until coconut toasts, about 30 minutes. Cool, cut into squares.

Makes about 18 squares.

## Chocolate Dipped Apricots

6 ounces semi-sweet chocolate chips

24 large dried apricots

6 ounces white chocolate chips

Melt the semi-sweet chocolate in microwave or in pan over simmering water. Dip apricots 2/3 up and place on waxed paper lined tray. Chill in refrigerator. Melt white chocolate in the same fashion as dark, and dip the apricots 1/2 way up (a slight overlapping) so apricots are 1/2 white and 1/2 dark. Return to waxed paper lined tray and refrigerate.

Serves 12.

 ## White Star Mimosas

1 quart peach nectar

1 pint raspberries

1 bottle White Star or good Brut champagne

Divide the peach nectar and raspberries among 8 or 10 champagne flutes. Top with chilled champagne and serve.

Serves 8–10.

## Passion Fruit Blend

1/2 gallon passion fruit juice
1/8 cup grenadine (optional)
1 pint good vodka placed in freezer overnight

Mix together juice, grenadine, and vodka. Serve over ice or frozen fresh strawberry slices.

Serves 8–12.

## Iced Tea with Peach Ice Cubes

1 pitcher homemade iced tea of choice
enough peach nectar to fill up two trays of ice cubes (about 2 cups)
orange slices for garnish

Chill iced tea as you make cubes of peach nectar ice. Serve tea over peach cubes and garnish with orange slices.

Serves 4–6.

## Malibu Style Latke Fest

*Our first Chanukah in Malibu came upon us very quickly. We were still new to Malibu, and I had been taping shows since we arrived. I had been, however, written up in Florida for my latkes, and I thought perhaps it was time to take a breather and have a little gathering with some of our new California friends.*

We set some tables out on the deck, put on some sun glasses, and heated up the oil for the latkes. Before I knew it, the sun was setting, the ocean was calming, and the beach goers were going. We were having our first latke fest, Malibu style.

*chef harry & friends*

**Malibu Style**
**Latke Fest**

 — *hints* —

- The chutneys and humus can be made the day in advance.
- The salmon cakes can be made early in the day and reheated in the oven before serving.
- You can make the honey nut topping earlier, too.

# m • e • n • u

Feta and Calamatas

Hubris Humus

Bubbie's "Eet vont be da same vit out de schmaltz!" Latkes

Blue Cheese and Leek Chutney

Cinnamon Apple Chutney

Curried Salmon Cakes

Nutin', Honey

## Feta and Calamatas

8 ounces feta cheese, cut into small squares

1 cup Calamata olives, drained (and pitted if you are
   feeling energetic)

1 small red onion, sliced thinly

1 teaspoon dried oregano

2 tablespoons extra virgin olive oil

1 tablespoon fresh minced garlic

cracked pepper to taste

Arrange the cheese and olives over the onion slices. Mix
together the oregano, oil, and garlic. Drizzle over cheese and
olives. Crack pepper over the top.

Serves 6–8.

 ## Hubris Humus

30 ounces prepared garbanzo beans, drained

8 cloves garlic

1 cup toasted sesame seeds

juice from 3 limes

1 teaspoon salt or to taste

1/3 cup rinsed fresh chopped parsley leaves

1 minced jalapeno pepper (Wear rubber gloves when handling
   hot peppers.)

1 cup extra virgin olive oil

Puree the garbanzos with the garlic, sesame, lime juice, salt,
parsley, and jalapeno, adding oil slowly to create a paste.

Makes about 3 cups.

*chef harry & friends*

*Malibu Style*
*Latke Fest*

—— *words of* ——
*appreciation*

*'Tanks' God, for our
beautiful lives, the happiness
of The Festival of Lights and
the laughter of children. Oye
Vay, please let this heartburn
pass before bedtime!*

##  Bubbie's "Eet vont be da same vit out de schmaltz!" Latkes

4 cups shredded raw, peeled and washed potatoes

1 cup minced onion

salt and pepper to taste

5 eggs, slightly beaten

1/8 cup schmaltz (optional)

vegetable oil for frying

Mix potato with onion, salt, pepper, and eggs. Melt schmaltz with enough oil to make a 1/8-inch layer in the bottom of a large, nonstick, heavy sauté pan over medium-high heat. Spoon potato mixture into hot oil to create little pancakes, frying until very brown on both sides. Hold in warm oven on paper towel until all latkes are fried, adding more schmaltz and oil as needed.

Makes about 24 pancakes.

##  Blue Cheese and Leek Chutney

1 tablespoon extra virgin olive oil

2 leeks, trimmed, split, rinsed, and chopped

1 cup crumbled blue cheese

2 cups sour cream

1 teaspoon sweet paprika

1 teaspoon fresh minced garlic

salt and pepper to taste

Heat oil in a small skillet over medium heat and sauté leek until toasted, about 10 minutes. Cool and mix with balance of

ingredients. Season with salt and pepper. Cover and refrigerate until ready to serve.

Makes a generous 2 cups.

##  Cinnamon Apple Chutney

4 large apples, peeled, cored, and chunked

juice and zest from 2 limes

1 1/2 cups granulated sugar

1 teaspoon ground cinnamon

3 bananas, peeled and sliced

Place apples, lime juice and zest, sugar, and cinnamon in heavy saucepan over medium heat. When contents begins to simmer, stir and reduce heat to medium-low to simmer for 10 minutes. Stir in banana and simmer 2 minutes more. Pour into heat-proof glass or ceramic bowl and serve warm.

Makes about 3 cups.

##  Curried Salmon Cakes

16 ounces canned and drained or leftover poached salmon, bones and skin removed

1 cup diced purple or red bell pepper

1 cup minced scallions

1 cup plain bread crumbs

1/3 cup fat free yogurt

8 large egg whites or 4 large eggs

2 tablespoons (or to taste) mild curry powder or blend

*Malibu Style
Latke Fest*

1 teaspoon sweet paprika

1 tablespoon Dijon mustard

2 tablespoons sweet pickle relish

1 teaspoon Worcestershire sauce

salt and pepper to taste

butter or margarine for frying

Mix together ingredients except butter to combine well. Heat a large, heavy, nonstick skillet over high heat and melt in enough butter to coat the bottom generously. Spoon patties into pan and shape gently as you go. Brown on both sides and fry until done, about 3 or 4 minutes per side. Keep warm in oven until all cakes are fried.

Makes about 12 3-inch cakes or 24 bite-sized appetizer cakes.

## Nutin', Honey

2 cups slivered almonds

1 cup granulated sugar

1 teaspoon cinnamon

1 cup raisins

vanilla ice cream

honey

Heat and stir the almonds and sugar in a nonstick sauté pan over medium-high heat until sugar melts and adheres to almonds and almonds brown. Sprinkle with cinnamon, spread on waxed or parchment paper, and cool. Toss with raisins and serve over scoops of ice cream. Drizzle with honey.

Makes enough for 6–8 servings.

# Dinner on the Dume with Jackie Zeman Gordon

*Jackie Zeman Gordan appears on General Hospital almost five days a week, and the limousine picks her up before the sun comes up. She works hard and returns to the gated Malibu estate on posh Pointe Dume as though returning from an errand. Her sharp and hospitable husband, Glen, and two gorgeous daughters paint a beautiful family picture with Jackie as the centerpiece.*

Their rambling Mediterranean home is casually splendid and dotted with charming crafts created by the girls. Jackie only wanted to talk about Italian food, and she knew exactly how she wanted things to be. We were joined by some mutual friends, and the gathering was full of warmth and, well, if I do say so myself, great food. It was a pleasure getting to know the family, and we have become friends. Only knowing each other a short time, we already have fond memories to share when we bump into each other around Malibu.

chef harry & friends

*Dinner on the Dume with Jackie Zeman Gordon*

— hints —

- Make the pate, crostini, vinaigrette, and truffles the day before.
- The veal can be assembled early in the day and baked off just before serving, as can the pasta cakes.
- Serve the truffles on dinner-sized plates and garnish with a rose for a very dramatic effect.

# m • e • n • u

Roasted Elephant Garlic Pate

Gorgonzola Bruschetta

Olive Bread Crostini

Organic Baby Greens with Toasted Walnut and Spring Onion Vinaigrette

Garlic Crusted Veal Escallop à la Vodka

Pasta Cakes with Roasted Peppers and Basil

Sauté of Fresh Greens and Garlic

Chocolate Truffles in Raspberry Chantilly Cream

## Roasted Elephant Garlic Pate

6 heads elephant garlic

3 tablespoons extra virgin olive oil

salt and pepper to taste

Trim the heads off the garlic to show just the tops of the cloves and drizzle with 1 tablespoon of the olive oil. Wrap loosely in aluminum foil and roast in preheated 325 degree oven for 2 hours or until garlic is very soft. Allow to cool until you can squeeze the softened cloves from the peel into a dish and mash with remaining oil. Season with salt and pepper to taste. Serve with crusty bread or rosemary focaccia.

Serves 4–6.

 ## Gorgonzola Bruschetta

4 cups chopped seeded firm tomato

1 tablespoon extra virgin olive oil

2 tablespoons fresh minced garlic

1 tablespoon red wine vinegar

1 cup fresh chopped rinsed basil leaves

1 cup crumbled Gorgonzola cheese

cracked pepper to taste

Toss together all ingredients to combine and divide among warm Olive Bread Crostini.

Serves 10–12.

—— *words of* ——
*appreciation*

*Children frolicking
in the grass, roses blooming
in the sun, and water,
trickling over rocks in a
stream, our world is one of
immeasurable beauty. We
give thanks for that bestowed
upon us and our loved ones.*

## Olive Bread Crostini

2 sticks butter

1/8 cup fresh minced garlic

1 loaf olive bread, sliced into 1/2-inch thick pieces and then into
   halves or thirds for appetizer sizes, about 24 crostini in all

Melt butter in saucepan over medium-high heat and stir in garlic to cook for 1 minute. Brush garlic butter on bottom of baking trays, and arrange bread on top. Paint tops of olive bread slices with remaining garlic butter. Bake in preheated 350 degree oven for 15 minutes, reduce heat to 200 degrees, and crisp, about 1 hour. Serve warm.

Serves 10–12.

 ## Organic Baby Greens with Toasted Walnut and Spring Onion Vinaigrette

1 tablespoon safflower oil

2 tablespoons fresh minced garlic

1 cup walnut pieces

1/2 cup fresh chopped basil leaves

1 cup chopped spring onions
   or scallions

2/3 cup red wine vinegar

1 tablespoon granulated sugar
   or more to taste

2/3 cup extra virgin olive oil

salt and pepper to taste

16 to 20 ounces baby salad
   greens (organic, if possible)

6 olive crostini, crushed

1 cup shredded Parmesan
   cheese

Heat safflower oil in heavy skillet over medium-high heat until hot. Stir in garlic and walnuts and sauté while stirring until walnuts begin to toast and turn golden. Remove from heat and allow to stand 10 minutes. Stir in basil, onions, vinegar, sugar, olive oil, salt, and pepper. Taste, and adjust seasoning if necessary. Toss greens with dressing, crostini, and Parmesan.

Serves 8.

## Garlic Crusted Veal Escallop à la Vodka

*For the escallop:*

2 pounds thinly pounded veal scallopini

6 egg whites, slightly beaten

1/2 cup drinking sherry

4 cups bread crumbs

1 tablespoon dried oregano

1 tablespoon dried basil

1 tablespoon salt

1 tablespoon fresh pepper

extra virgin olive oil for frying

1/8 cup fresh minced garlic

Place the veal in a bowl with the egg whites and sherry. Mix well and allow to marinate 30 minutes. Mix together the bread crumbs with the oregano, basil, salt, and pepper, and dredge each piece of veal in the crumbs to coat.

Heat 1/8-inch layer of oil in a heavy, large, nonstick sauté pan over medium-high heat and stir in 1/3 of the minced garlic. Arrange pieces of veal in the hot oil and brown 90 seconds on each side. Drain and finish with the remaining pieces adding more garlic and oil as needed.

*For the sauce:*

2 sticks butter

3 tablespoons fresh minced garlic

1 cup fresh minced onion

1 cup fresh minced basil

1 tablespoon dried oregano

1/4 cup red wine

1/4 cup vodka

30 ounces tomato puree

3 tablespoons granulated sugar

1 pint heavy cream

1 cup grated Parmesan

crushed red pepper to taste (optional)

Heat butter in large, heavy saucepan over medium-high heat and stir in garlic and onion. Sauté for 4 minutes. Stir in basil and oregano and sauté 1 minute more. Stir in wine and vodka, reduce heat to medium, and stir in puree and sugar. When mixture begins to simmer, stir in cream and cheese. Stir until cheese melts and sauce is creamy.

*To assemble:*

2 cups shredded mozzarella cheese

2 cups shredded fontina cheese

Place 1 cup of sauce in each of the bottom of two baking dishes that accommodate veal pieces in one layer. They may touch each other. Ladle sauce over veal, and divide cheeses over the top. Bake in preheated 350 degree oven until cheese is bubbly and browned.

Serves 8–10.

## Pasta Cakes with Roasted Peppers and Basil

1½ pounds boiled spaghetti, cooled and cut a few times to shorten
    lengths randomly

6 eggs

1 tablespoon fresh minced garlic

2 cups chopped roasted or grilled red peppers

1 cup fresh chopped basil leaves

salt and pepper to taste

Mix pasta with eggs, garlic, peppers, basil, salt, and pepper. Divide among 12 greased muffin tins. Bake in preheated 350 degree oven until puffy and golden on the top, about 30 minutes.

Makes 12 cakes.

## Sauté of Fresh Greens and Garlic

3 tablespoons extra virgin olive oil

1/4 cup thinly sliced garlic

12 ounces rinsed fresh baby spinach leaves

8 ounces fresh arugula

1 tablespoon soy sauce

cracked pepper to taste

Heat oil in large stock pot over medium-high heat and stir in garlic. Sauté until golden brown and stir in greens until slightly wilted, about 90 seconds. Drizzle with soy sauce and pepper and stir. Serve immediately.

Serves 6.

 ## Chocolate Truffles in Raspberry Chantilly Cream

*For the truffle batter:*

1 quart heavy whipping cream

2 cups sugar

1 cup cocoa powder

8 ounces broken gourmet dark chocolate bar

1 stick butter softened

In a large, heavy saucepan over medium heat, stir cream and sugar until cream begins to simmer. Stir in cocoa powder, and simmer mixture for 25 minutes, stirring occasionally and keeping heat low enough to prevent scalding. Remove from heat and stir in chocolate pieces to melt. Place a small mixing bowl into a larger bowl of ice. Pour batter into small mixing bowl and beat with electric hand mixer until cool and beginning to thicken. Beat in butter until smooth and place in refrigerator covered with plastic wrap directly on batter. Chill overnight.

*To make truffles:*

1 cup powdered sugar

1 cup cocoa powder

1 tablespoon cinnamon powder

Mix ingredients together, and drop spoonfuls of batter into sweetened cocoa mixture and quickly roll to shape and coat. Remove to tray lined with waxed paper. Chill until ready to serve.

Makes 24 truffles.

*For Raspberry Chantilly Cream:*

| | |
|---|---|
| 1 pint heavy whipping cream | 2 tablespoons raspberry preserves |
| 1/2 cup powdered sugar | fresh raspberries for garnish |
| 1 teaspoon vanilla extract | |

Whip the cream with electric beater in chilled bowl, and gradually add sugar continuing to beat until stiff peaks are formed. Beat in vanilla and raspberry preserves.

*To Serve:*

Divide cream among serving plates, and arrange truffles in "pools" of cream. Garnish with fresh raspberries.

Enough for 8–10 servings.

# Seaside Supper on the Grill

When we lived on glorious Jupiter Island in Hobe Sound, Florida we had a little gazebo right on the sand that, at high tide, could be "kissed" by the water. That little spot is really what sold us on the property. We had this fabulous grill/smoker combination, and I put it out by that Gazebo as soon as it came off the moving van. With the picnic table centered under the peak of the gazebo's roof, we had an instant party on the beach. A bag of coals, a cooler full of fixings, our daughter's sea glass and shell finds decorating the table; before long we developed a routine that allowed an entire meal made on the grill, beachside and sunshaded. It was almost as though the boats sailed by for our entertainment. P.S. Always remember: making dinner outside on the grill means very little cleanup in the kitchen!

chef harry & friends

*Seaside Supper
on the Grill*

——— *h i n t s* ———

- Make the polenta the day before and grill with the asparagus and sea scallops.
- The chutney, vinaigrette, and rosemary butter can be made the day in advance.

# m • e • n • u

Grilled Polenta

Garlic Basil Chutney

Balsamic Gorgonzola Vinaigrette over
Grilled Romaine Hearts

Grilled Asparagus with Rosemary Butter

Grilled Sea Scallops

Watermelon Sorbet

## Grilled Polenta

1 recipe polenta, (page 178)
garlic flavored olive oil

Cut polenta into desired shapes and paint with oil. Grill over medium-hot coals until hot, about 90 seconds per side. Serve warm.

Serves 4–6.

## Garlic Basil Chutney

2 tablespoons extra virgin olive oil
1 cup minced onion
1/4 cup fresh peeled garlic cloves
2 cups fresh basil leaves
salt and pepper to taste

Heat oil in heavy, nonstick sauté pan over medium-high heat and stir in onion and garlic. Reduce heat to medium-low and cook until garlic is tender, about 25 minutes. Cool and puree in food processor fitted with steel blade until smooth. Add basil and pulse to chop into a chutney texture. Season with salt and pepper.

Makes about 2 cups.

—— *words of* ——
*appreciation*

*The ocean breeze
tussling the hair of a child
as it does the leaves of a
palm, the pelican sitting and
waiting for a meal, the turtle
ashore to lay her eggs, we
are lost in a sea of beauty
and wonderment.*

# Balsamic Gorgonzola Vinaigrette over Grilled Romaine Hearts

*For the vinaigrette:*

2/3 cup balsamic vinegar

1/2 cup extra virgin olive oil

1 teaspoon fresh minced garlic

1 teaspoon dried oregano or 1 tablespoon fresh minced

1/4 cup fresh minced basil

1 cup crumbled Gorgonzola cheese

1 tablespoon granulated sugar

fresh cracked pepper to taste

Mix together well. Cover and refrigerate until ready to use. Bring to room temperature to serve.

*To grill romaine hearts:*

4 romaine hearts, split in two halves and rinsed thoroughly

1/8 cup extra virgin olive oil

1 teaspoon fresh minced garlic

Pat romaine dry, and mix oil with garlic. Brush oil over cut sides of hearts. Grill hearts cut side down over hot coals for 1 minutes. Remove to serving platter or plates, and spoon dressing over warm lettuce.

Serves 8.

Rosemary Butter

2 sticks butter, softened to room temperature

1 tablespoon fresh minced rosemary, stems removed

salt and pepper to taste

Mix together and serve room temperature. May be refrigerated up to 3 days before using.

Makes 1/2 cup.

 Grilled Asparagus

2 pounds young asparagus, trimmed and rinsed

1 gallon salted boiling water

2 tablespoons extra virgin olive oil

1 teaspoon fresh minced garlic

1 teaspoon soy sauce

Place asparagus in a heat-proof colander in the sink. Pour boiling water over to blanch. Mix together the oil, garlic, and soy sauce. Toss with asparagus, and grill asparagus over medium-hot coals until tender, about 3 minutes. Serve hot with Rosemary Butter.

Serves 6–8.

 # Grilled Sea Scallops

2 pounds large fresh sea scallops

2 tablespoons soy sauce

2 tablespoons extra virgin olive oil

1 tablespoon fresh minced garlic

juice from 1 lime

1 teaspoon powdered ginger

Rinse scallops and drain. Mix together soy sauce, oil, garlic, lime juice, and ginger. Marinate scallops in mixture up to 4 hours. Grill over medium-hot coals until just done, about 90 seconds per side or scallops are no longer pink inside.

Serves 8.

 # Watermelon Sorbet

1/3 to 1/2 fresh seedless watermelon or watermelon flesh with
    seeds removed; enough for 5 to 6 cups of puree

1/2 cup powdered sugar

Puree melon and sugar in food processor and place in ice cream machine or sorbet maker. Freeze according to manufacturer's directions. Serve immediately.

Serves 8–10.

# Coochi Coochi Ribs in Reno with Charro

*Charro lit up the kitchen at John Ascuaga's Nugget in Reno Nevada like a full moon on a crisp fall night. Waving at admirers and throwing kisses to the sous chefs, I knew I was in for some fun. I had been invited to Reno by John Ascuaga's to be a judge in the "Best of the West Rib Cookoff." It was a tough job, but somebody had to do it. When we found out that Charro was performing at the Hotel, it sounded like a show in the making.*

Seems Charro's homebase is Hawaii where she does some south of the border cooking at a very successful restaurant of her own. No wonder she was right at home in the kitchen of a place that can serve eight or ten thousand meals in a day. Everyone stood back as I made my ribs that were briefly famous in Tulsa, Oklahoma where I created them. Charro licked her fingers and gave me a "Coochi Coochi" and that was enough for me!

Coochi Coochi
Ribs in Reno
with Charro

─── *hints* ───

- Make the slaw and the
  pie the day before. Buy
  some smoked ribs from
  your favorite barbecue
  joint and glaze them
  yourself. You can have a
  fast, easy, and fabulous
  picnic in a flash.

# m · e · n · u

Amish Slaw

Sesame Glazed Spareribs

Ice Cream Pie

## Amish Slaw

1 pound finely shredded white cabbage—the prepackaged kind in
  the market is great

1½ cups mayonnaise

1/4 cup red wine vinegar

2 tablespoons celery seed

2/3 cup milk or cream

2 tablespoons granulated sugar

salt and pepper to taste

Rinse cabbage and drain. Mix together mayonnaise, vinegar, celery seed, milk, and sugar until smooth. Season with salt and pepper and pour over cabbage. Refrigerate 1 hour or up to 24 hours before serving.

Serves 4–6.

## Sesame Glazed Spareribs

3 racks smoked spareribs, cut into individual ribs

2 cups granulated sugar

1/4 cup soy sauce

1/3 cup fresh minced garlic

1/4 cup fresh minced ginger

1/3 cup toasted sesame seeds

Place ribs in roasting pan in 275 degree oven and roast, uncovered, while making glaze. To make glaze: heat sugar and soy

—— *words of* ——
*appreciation*

*There are times in life when*
*we must close our eyes*
*to make sure we are not*
*dreaming. May those times*
*be of what dreams are made.*

sauce in heavy saucepan over medium-high heat until it begins to simmer. Boil gently for 15 minutes. Stir in garlic and ginger and boil 2 minutes more. Pour over ribs and toss to coat. Sprinkle with sesame seeds and serve.

Serves 8 as an appetizer or 4 for dinner.

# Ice Cream Pie

12 ounces creme-filled chocolate sandwich cookies (like Oreos)

1 stick butter, softened

10 ounces caramel sauce

1 pint vanilla ice cream, softened

1 cup crushed toffee

1 pint chocolate ice cream, softened

whipped topping

chocolate sprinkles

Pulse cookies and butter in food processor fitted with steel blade, until texture of coarse meal. Press to cover bottom and sides of pie pan in an even layer. Cover bottom with caramel sauce, and spoon vanilla ice cream over caramel. Sprinkle toffee over that. Refreeze. Spoon chocolate ice cream over frozen pie and refreeze. Allow to stand 20 minutes before topping with whipped topping and sprinkling with chocolate sprinkles.

Serves 8–12.

# Standing Room Only: The Cocktail Buffet

*This, without a doubt, is my favorite kind of party. It is a gathering of people who we choose and a wide variety of food attractively arranged as the focal point for an evening. I try to hire someone to care for the beverages so I can stand there with Laurie and just enjoy myself (someone to help clean up wouldn't be bad, either). It is the perfect way to entertain a large group of people for dinner, without pulling out your hair and spending a fortune by renting tables, chairs, cloths, and maybe even a tent! The time always goes by too quickly, and I find I have just been to a fabulous party and did not have to drive home.*

I try and make a lot of different things for our guests to sample. A good friend coined the phrase "gourmet grazing," and that is what this is always about. The more variety the better. People should have a plate and a fork and have a meal by just generously sampling many things. I make sure their is a selection of nibbles, a salad or two, some entree items (everything should be able to be eaten without the use of a knife), and I often put desserts at a station somewhere else in the room or even another part of the house if we are having lots and lots of people.

Do not hesitate to add to your selection with some catered or favorite purchased creations. It is no sin to buy a rich cheesecake or a couple dozen imported chocolates to enhance the desserts. Bowls of fresh berries, some luscious chocolate truffles, and sweet cheeses are an elegant, easy, and delicious sweet station—not a bad combination. Make this kind of party easy and fun. Take a shower and relax an hour before the guests are to arrive. Be organized, plan ahead, and have a ball!

## chef harry & friends

*Standing Room Only: The Cocktail Buffet*

### — hints —

- While there are a lot of selections here, nothing is too tough to make.
- The toasts, brisket, salsa, grapes, and Cashew Brittle can be made the day ahead.
- Toast the ravioli a few hours before the party and keep it warm in the oven.
- The salmon platter can be prepared early in the day, covered, and refrigerated until ready to serve.
- Put the pump rolls in a linen lined basket, and the brisket in a chaffing dish.

# m • e • n • u

## (for 18–24 guests)

Texas Goat Cheese with Garlic and Basil

Smoked Salmon with Cumin, Lime, and Chili

Parmesan Toasts

Barbecue of Brisket on Mini Pump Rolls

Toasted Spinach Ravioli

Garlic Marinated Mussels

Eggplant Tomato Salsa

Chocolate Dipped Grape Clusters

Cashew Brittle

## Texas Goat Cheese with Garlic and Basil

24 ounces fresh goat cheese

1/2 cup extra virgin olive oil

1 tablespoon fresh minced garlic

1 minced sweet green chili pepper

1 minced seeded jalapeno

1 cup fresh chopped basil leaves

salt and fresh cracked pepper to taste

Crumble goat cheese over heat-proof serving platter. Heat oil in heavy saucepan over medium-high heat and stir in garlic and peppers. Sauté 5 minutes. Remove from heat and let stand 10 minutes. Stir in basil and drizzle over cheese. Sprinkle with salt and pepper and serve with warm small tortillas, chips, or toasts.

Serves 18–24 as part of buffet.

## Smoked Salmon with Cumin, Lime, and Chili

2 pounds smoked salmon, thinly sliced

4 limes

1/4 cup ground cumin

1 tablespoon medium-hot chili powder

4 seeded and chopped firm tomatoes

1 minced onion

1/2 cup fresh chopped cilantro leaves

juice from 1 lemon

—— *words of* ——
*appreciation*

*We are so very thankful for our many blessings. May we be so fortunate as to gather together again soon to enjoy life in good health!*

Arrange slices on serving platter. Squeeze lime juice over salmon. Mix cumin and chili powder and sprinkle over salmon evenly. Mix together tomato, onion, cilantro, and lemon juice. Serve with salmon as a garnish.

Serves 18–24 as part of buffet.

 ## Parmesan Toasts

1 pound butter

1/8 cup fresh minced garlic

1 tablespoon salt

2 loaves party cocktail rye bread

2 cups shredded Parmesan

Melt butter in heavy saucepan over medium-high heat. Stir in garlic and salt. Paint baking sheets to accommodate bread slices in 1 layer with garlic butter, and arrange bread slices on top, doing in batches, if necessary. Paint tops with garlic butter and sprinkle with cheese. Bake in preheated 325 degree oven for 25 minutes, and reduce heat to 200 degrees to crisp.

Serves 18–24 as part of buffet.

 ## Barbecue of Brisket on Mini Pump Rolls

1 large brisket, trimmed

4 cups water

2 bay leaves

1 pint barbecue sauce of choice

2 large white onions, sliced in thick slices

2 tablespoons pepper

1 tablespoon paprika

1/2 cup prepared horseradish

36 to 42 small split pump or French rolls

4 tablespoons kosher salt

Rinse brisket. Place onion slices in bottom of roasting pan, and place brisket on top of onions. Pour water over brisket, and place bay leaves in water. Sprinkle brisket with salt, pepper, and paprika. Cover pan tightly with foil to seal and bake in preheated 300 degree oven for 6 hours. Remove from oven, and when cool enough to handle, trim fat from brisket and chop meat. Place meat in a baking dish or casserole. Mix the barbecue sauce with the horse-radish and 1 cup of juice from the brisket roasting pan and pour over brisket. Keep hot and covered in oven. Serve warm on buns.

Serves 18–24 as part of buffet.

## Toasted Spinach Ravioli

42 premade fresh cheese filled spinach ravioli, cooked and cooled

8 eggs, lightly beaten

2 cups bread crumbs

1/4 cup fresh minced garlic

butter for sautéing

Place the cooked ravioli in a bowl with the eggs and gently toss to coat. Dredge ravioli in crumbs. Place 1/4 of the minced gar-lic with enough butter to form a generous layer on the bottom of

227

a large, heavy, nonstick sauté pan over medium-high heat, and sauté ravioli until brown and crisp on both sides, about 3 minutes per side. Repeat in 3 more batches and hold on ravioli trays in warm oven until ready to serve.

Serves 18–24 as part of buffet.

 ## Garlic Marinated Mussels

2 pounds fresh smoked mussels (if using canned mussels, drain)
2 tablespoons fresh minced garlic
1/2 cup chopped basil leaves
1/4 cup minced parsley
fresh cracked pepper to taste
1/4 cup extra virgin olive oil

Place mussels in a glass or ceramic bowl. Mix together the garlic, basil, parsley, pepper, and oil and toss with mussels. Marinate up to 24 hours. (You may also warm marinated mussels and toss with fresh cooked pasta for an incredible meal!)

Serves 18–24 as part of buffet.

 ## Eggplant Tomato Salsa

2 medium eggplants
1/4 cup plus 2 tablespoons extra virgin olive oil
2 tablespoons fresh minced garlic
1 tablespoon soy sauce
4 chopped seeded tomatoes

1 tablespoon dried oregano

1/2 cup fresh chopped basil leaves

1 cup minced onion

1 cup chopped roasted red pepper

1/4 cup fresh chopped parsley

salt and pepper to taste

Slice the eggplant into 1-inch thick slices. Mix the 1/4 cup olive oil with 1 tablespoon of the garlic and the soy sauce, and toss the eggplant with the mixture to coat. Grill eggplant over medium-hot coals until tender, about 3 minutes per side. Cool and chop. Mix with balance of ingredients and remaining 2 tablespoons olive oil. Season with salt and pepper.

Serves 18–24 as part of buffet.

## Chocolate Dipped Grape Clusters

2 pounds seedless grapes

12 ounces dark or white chocolate chips

Rinse grapes and dry on paper towels. Snip into clusters of 4 to 6 grapes each. Melt chocolate in microwave or in pan set over another pan containing simmering water.

Dip tips of grape clusters in melted chocolate and place on wax paper lined trays. Refrigerate to harden up to 24 hours before serving.

Serves 8–12.

# Cashew Brittle

1 ½ pounds salted cashews

4 cups granulated sugar

1 cup light Karo syrup

1 cup water

4 tablespoons butter, cut into bits

2 teaspoons baking soda

Spread cashews in an even layer on a buttered jelly roll pan. Stir sugar, syrup, and water in large, heavy saucepan or Dutch oven over medium-high heat to combine, and allow contents to boil softly. Reduce heat to maintain boil and cook to very golden brown (hard crack on candy thermometer) about 25 minutes or so. Turn off heat and stir in butter and baking soda. Caution: When the baking soda is stirred in, the mixture foams up quickly and settles down! Pour over cashews and allow to cool and harden. Break into pieces to serve.

Serves 10–12

# Index
# By Course

*chef harry & friends*

———— c o u r s e s ————

Appetizers . . . . . . . 231

Breads . . . . . . . . . 232

Salads . . . . . . . . . 232

Condiments,
   Salsas,
   and Sauces . . . . 233

Side Dishes,
   Vegetables,
   and Pasta . . . . . 234

Sandwiches . . . . . . 235

Entrees . . . . . . . . 235

Desserts . . . . . . . 235

Beverages . . . . . . . 236

## APPETIZERS

Antipasto, Grand, 171

Artichoke Nachos, 19

Baked Artichoke Parmesan Dip, 119

Baked Brie in Filo, 183

Baked Tortilla Chips, 66

Cello Noodle and Cabbage Spring Rolls, 81

Chicken Nam Sod, 163

Cilantro Pickled Shellfish, 65

Curried Cucumber and Caper Chutney in Belgian
   Endive Leaves, 95

Curried Garbanzo Pate, 25

Curried Pickled Fish, 109

Drunken Seafood Medley, 95

Fermented Black Bean Tapenade with
   Fried Won Tons, 83

Feta and Calamatas, 199

Four Season Chips, 20

Garlic Baked Salami, 104

Garlic Marinated Mussels, 228

Genoa Marinated Shrimp, 173

Gorgonzola Bruschetta, 205

Grecian Finger Sandwiches, 189

Grilled Calamari, 173

Grilled Marinated Peppers, 174

Grilled Scallions, 175

Grilled Tomatoes and
   Parmesan, 174

Hubris Humus, 199

Marinated Asiago, 171

Mozzarella with Pesto, 171

Mozzarella with Sun Dried
   Tomato, 172

Pan Fried Dumplings, 163

Pate of Mediterranean Olives,
   Capers, and Garlic, 135

Popcorn Shrimp Bruschetta, 33

Prosciutto Wrapped Figs, 171

Quick Crudité, 103

Roasted Elephant Garlic Pate, 205

Shrimp and Fresh Dill in
   Ouzo, 156

Shrimp and Spinach Filo Spring
   Rolls, 11

Smoked Salmon Bruschetta, 96

Smoked Salmon with Cumin,
   Lime, and Chili, 225

Sun Dried Tomatoes and Sonoma
   Goat Cheese Grape Leaf
   Cigars, 12

Sweet Potato Coconut Soup
   with Wild Boar Blueberry
   Sausage, 110

Texas Goat Cheese with Garlic
   and Basil, 225

Tiny Marinated Grilled Lamb
   Chops, 155

Wasabi Teriyaki Nuts, 81

## BREADS

Garlic Crostini, 33

Herbed Flatbreads, 25

Jalapeno Corn Bread, 143

Olive Bread Crostini, 206

Parmesan Toasts, 226

Sautéed Corn Pepper Bread, 114

## SALADS

Amish Slaw, 221

Arugula and Radicchio with
   Pistachio Gorgonzola
   Vinaigrette, 177

Baby Greens with Crab and Toasted
   Almond Vinaigrette, 183

Basil Lentil Salad, 130

Black Bean and Corn Salad, 91

Bocconcini and Mini Multi-
   Colored Tomato Salad, 191

Bold Coast Pasta Salad, 150

Chopped Caesar Salad, 156

Corn Pepper Relish and Greens, 55

Corn Pepper Relish with Fresh Lemon Thyme, 189

Italian Greens, Purple Grapes, and Blue Goat Cheese with Toasted Pecan Vinaigrette, 96

Mango Chile Chutney with Baby Greens, 76

Mixed Baby Greens and Asparagus with Raspberry Vinaigrette, 12

Mixed Greens and Mango with Papaya Seed Vinaigrette, 28

New Potatoes with Dilled Shallot Vinaigrette, 54

Organic Baby Greens with Toasted Walnut and Spring Onion Vinaigrette, 206

Pink Lentil Salad, 190

Quick Maine Bread and Butter Pickles, 149

Salad of Pickled Chopped Beet, Green Beans, and Onion, 111

Toasted Garlic Vinaigrette with Mixed Italian Greens, 135

Wild Rice Salad, 40

Yellow Tomato and Jicama Salad with Toasted Pepitas, 68

## CONDIMENTS, SALSAS, AND SAUCES

Apricot, Date, and Vidalia Chutney, 113

Apricot Mint Dipping Sauce, 155

Balsamic Gorgonzola Vinaigrette, 200

Blue Cheese and Leek Chutney, 208

Cilantro Chili Butter, 144

Cinnamon Apple Chutney, 201

Coconut Currant Chutney, 98

Corn Cumin Relish, 67

Cranberry Jalapeno Salsa, 120

Cranberry Mint Chutney, 13

Curried Lemon Dipping Sauce, 141

Dijon Dipping Sauce, 103

Eggplant Tomato Salsa, 228

Garlic Basil Chutney, 215

Garlic Peppered Dipping Sauce, 47

Peppered Garlic Aioli, 26

Peppered Peanut Dipping Sauce, 82

Quick Curry Dipping Sauce, 76

Quick White Salsa, 89

Roasted Garlic and Cubanelle Pepper Coulis, 65

Rosemary Butter, 217

Salsa Diablo, 20

Salsa Las Virgenes, 19

Sesame Scallion Dipping Sauce, 164

Shallot Sesame Sour Cream
Chutney, 131

Warm Apple Cinnamon
Chutney, 60

# SIDE DISHES, VEGETABLES, AND PASTA

Angel Hair Pasta with Fresh
Tomatoes, Basil, and Garlic, 77

Angel Hair Pasta with Garlic
Crusted Sardines and Toasted
Almond Crumbs, 175

Bacon Gorgonzola Spinach, 34

Brown Rice with Scallions, 90

Bubbie's "Eet vont be da same vit
out de schmaltz!" Latkes, 200

Cheese Grits with Fresh Corn and
Green Chilies, 48

Corn Dressing Fritters, 121

Curried Sesame Yams with
Apricot Glaze, 84

Dutch Style Cabbage with
Granny Smith Apples, 113

Fried Okra, 47

Grilled Asparagus, 217

Grilled Eggplant and Goat
Cheese, 129

Grilled Polenta, 215

Grilled Portobellos, 136

Grilled Romaine Hearts, 216

Grilled Torpedo Onions, 14

Grilled Yellow Squash, 48

Leek Pudding, 99

Pasta Cakes with Roasted Peppers
and Basil, 209

Pinto Beans with Plantains and
Cilantro, 70

Pretty in Pink Pasta, 184

Rice with Cranberries, 158

Roasted Pepper Lasagna à la
Vodka, 136

Roasted Pepper Polenta, 178

Rosemary Roasted Potatoes, 60

Sautéed Mushrooms, 34

Sauté of California Olives, Organic
Fennel, and Rosemary, 15

Sauté of Fresh Greens and
Garlic, 210

Shrimp Studded Potato
Pancakes, 131

Spiced Pumpkin Pancakes, 59

Szechwan Green Beans, 165

Texmati Rice with Pinons, 21

Toasted Rice with Sprouts, Saffron, Red Pepper, and Mint, 85

Toasted Spinach Ravioli, 227

Whole Poached Artichokes, 27

## SANDWICHES

Barbecue of Brisket on Mini Pump Rolls, 226

Beef Tenderloin Club, 126

Caesar Salad Sandwich, 125

Coastal Crab Roll, 149

Grilled Chicken and Guacamole Subs, 104

## ENTREES

Apricot Shallot Glazed Pork, 97

Black Bean Turkey Burritos, 119

Cajun Soft Shell Crabs, 75

Chicken Fajitas, 89

Chicken Tamale Bake with Jalapeno Smashed Potatoes, 69

Chili Blackened Sole, 66

Crab Cakes with Red Peppers, 141

Curried Salmon Cakes, 201

Garlic Crusted Fried Chicken, 55

Garlic Crusted Veal Escallop à la Vodka, 207

Glazed Cornish Hens, 157

Glazed Tenderloin of Ostrich, 112

Grilled New York Strip Steak, 35

Grilled Sea Scallops, 218

Grilled Shrimp in Apricot Hoisin Sesame Glaze, 191

Grilled Shrimp Tandoori Style, 54

Herb Marinated Sonoma Lamb Chops, 14

Home Style Beef with Peanuts, 166

Lobster and Goat Cheese Quesadillas, 21

Peanut Sesame Tofu with Scallions, 83

Peppered Shrimp, 49

Pico de Gallo, 71

Seafood Scampi, 178

Sesame Glazed Spareribs, 221

Turkey Chili, 142

Vegetable Strudel, 39

## DESSERTS

Apple Lemon Loaf, 50

Blonde Brownies and Berries, 185

Brandied Coconut Custard with Currants, 115

Cashew Brittle, 230

Chocolate Dipped Apricots, 194

Chocolate Dipped Grape
    Clusters, 229

Chocolate Mascarpone Torte, 179

Chocolate Peanut Butter
    Meltaways, 106

Chocolate Plantain Cake, 28

Chocolate Truffles in Raspberry
    Chantilly Cream, 210

Cinnamon Chocolate Strawberry
    Mousse, 22

Cinnamon Meringues with Fresh
    Strawberry Sauce, 71

Citrus Zabaglione, 138

Coconut Almond Butterscotch
    Meltaways, 194

Coconut Sorbet, 86

Double Chocolate Brownies, 193

Dutch Apple Cake, 159

French Apple Cake, 40

Fresh Figs and Organic
    Raspberries, 192

Fresh Fruit Tarts, 126

Hazelnut White Chocolate
    Squares, 193

Ice Cream Pie, 222

Mandarin Pineapple Upside Down
    Cake, 167

Nutin', Honey, 202

Orange Apple Crumble, 144

Papaya Marshmallow Parfait, 91

Peach Crumble, 36

Pecan Praline Raspberry
    Cream, 132

Pecan Praline Tiramisu, 100

Pick Your Own Blueberry
    Crisp, 150

Raspberry Blueberry Crumble à la
    Mode, 56

Raspberry Citrus Sundae, 78

Raspberry Mascarpone Almond
    Tart, 16

Raspberry Mousse Parfaits, 121

Watermelon Sorbet, 218

## BEVERAGES

Berry Yogurt Velvet, 59

Cranberry Coolers, 53

Glacier Vodka, 53

Hot Chocolate, 61

Iced Tea with Peach Ice Cubes, 196

Lupine Honey Bee Tea, 151

Morning Chai, 42

Passion Fruit Blend, 196

White Star Mimosas, 195

# Index A–Z

## A

Aioli, Peppered Garlic, 26

Apple
  Dutch Cake, 159
  French Cake, 40
  Lemon Loaf, 50
  Orange Crumble, 144

Apricot Mint Dipping Sauce, 155

Artichoke
  Baked Parmesan Dip, 119
  Nachos, 19
  Whole Poached, 27

Arugula and Radicchio with Pistachio Gorgonzola
  Vinaigrette, 177

Asiago, Marinated, 171

Asparagus, Grilled with Rosemary Butter, 217

## B

Beans
  Black with Corn Salad, 91
  Fermented Black Tapenade with Fried
    Won Tons, 83
  Green, Szechwan, 165
  Pinto with Plantains and Cilantro, 70

Beef
  Brisket, Barbecued, 226
  Home Style with Peanuts, 166

Steak, Grilled New York
    Strip, 35
Tenderloin Club Sandwich, 126
Beets, in Salad of Pickled
    Chopped Vegetables, 111
Blueberry Crisp, 150
Bocconcini and Mini Multi-
    Colored Tomato Salad, 191
Brie, Baked in Filo, 183
Brownies, Blonde, 185
Brownies, Double Chocolate, 193


C

Cabbage, Dutch Style with
    Apples, 113
Caesar Salad, Chopped, 156
Caesar Salad Sandwich, 125
Calamari, Grilled, 173
Cashew Brittle, 230
Cello Noodle and Cabbage
    Spring Rolls, 81
Chai, Morning, 42
Chicken
    Fajitas, 89
    Garlic Crusted, 55
    Grilled in Subs with
    Guacamole, 104
    Nam Sod, 163

Tamale Bake with Jalapeno
    Smashed Potatoes, 69
Chips, Four Season, 20
Chocolate
    Dipped Apricots, 194
    Dipped Grape Clusters, 229
    Hot, 61
    Mascarpone Torte, 179
    Peanut Butter Meltaways, 106
    Plantain Cake, 28
    Truffles in Raspberry Chantilly
        Cream, 210
Chutney
    Apricot, Date, and Vidalia, 113
    Blue Cheese and Leek, 200
    Cinnamon Apple, 201
    Coconut Currant, 98
    Cranberry Mint, 13
    Curried Cucumbers and Caper
        in Belgian Endive Leaves, 95
    Garlic Basil, 215
    Mango Chile, 76
    Shallot Sesame Sour Cream, 131
    Warm Apple Cinnamon, 60
Cilantro Chili Butter, 144
Cinnamon Chocolate Strawberry
    Mousse, 22
Coconut Almond Butterscotch
    Meltaways, 194
Coconut Sorbet, 86
Corn Bread, Sautéd Pepper, 114

Corn Bread with Jalapenos, 143

Corn Cumin Relish, 67

Cornish Hens, Glazed, 157

Corn Pepper Relish with Fresh
    Lemon Thyme, 189

Coulis, Roasted Garlic and
    Cubanelle Pepper, 65

Crab
    with Baby Greens and Toasted
        Almond Vinaigrette, 183
    Cakes with Red Peppers, 141
    Roll, 149
    Softshell Cajun Style, 75

Cranberry Coolers, 53

Cranberry Jalapeno Salsa, 120

Crostini
    Garlic, 33
    Olive, 206

Crudité, 103

Curried Lemon Dipping Sauce, 141

Curry Dipping Sauce, 76

Custard, Brandied Coconut with
    Currants, 115

## D

Dijon Dipping Sauce, 103

Dumplings, Asian Pan Fried, 163

## E

Eggplant, Grilled with Goat
    Cheese, 129

Eggplant Tomato Salsa, 228

## F

Fennel, Sautéed with Olives and
    Rosemary, 15

Feta and Calamatas, 199

Figs, Fresh with Raspberries, 192

Figs, Prosciutto Wrapped, 171

Finger Sandwiches, Grecian, 189

Fish, Curried Pickled, 109

Flatbreads, Herbed, 25

Fritters, Corn Dressing, 121

Fruit Tarts, 126

## G

Garbonzo, Curried Pate, 25

Garlic, Roasted Elephant Pate, 205

Garlic Crostini, 33

Garlic Peppered Dipping Sauce, 47

Goat Cheese, Texas with Garlic
    and Basil, 225

Gorgonzola, Balsamic
    Vinaigrette, 216

Gorgonzola Bruschetta, 205

Green Beans, Szechwan, 165

Greens

    with Asparagus and Raspberry
        Vinaigrette, 12

    with Corn Pepper Relish, 55

    with Mango and Papaya Seed
        Vinaigrette, 28

    with Purple Grapes and Blue
        Goat Cheese, 96

    Sautéed with Garlic, 210

    with Toasted Garlic
        Vinaigrette, 135

    with Toasted Walnut and
        Spring Onion Vinaigrette, 206

Grits, Cheese with Fresh Corn
    and Green Chilies, 48

## H

Hazelnut, White Chocolate
    Squares, 193

Humus, 199

## I

Ice Cream Pie, 222

## J

Jicama with Yellow Tomato and
    Toasted Pepitas, 68

## L

Lamb Chops, Marinated and
    Grilled, 14

Lamb Chop, Tiny Appetizers, 155

Leek Pudding, 99

Lentil Salad, Pink with Herbs, 190

Lentil Salad with Basil, 130

Lobster and Goat Cheese
    Quesadillas, 21

## M

Mandarin Pineapple Upside Down
    Cake, 167

Meringues, Cinnamon, 71

Mimosas, White Star, 195

Morning Chai, 42

Mousse, Cinnamon Chocolate
    Strawberry, 22

Mozzarella, Fresh with Pesto, 171

Mozzarella, Fresh with Sun Dried
    Tomatoes, 172

Mushrooms, Sautéed, 34

Mussels, Garlic Marinated, 228